PHILIP'S JUNIOR SCHOOL ATLAS

Philip's World Atlases are published in association with The Royal Geographical Society (with The Institute of British Geographers).

The Society was founded in 1830 and given a Royal Charter in 1859 for 'the advancement of geographical science'. Today it is a leading world centre for geographical learning – supporting education, teaching, research and expeditions, and promoting public understanding of the subject.

Further information about the Society and how to join may be found on its website at: www.rgs.org

Published in Great Britain by Philip's, a division of Octopus Publishing Group Limited, 2–4 Heron Quays, London E14 4JP

in association with Reed Primary, Halley Court, Jordan Hill, Oxford OX2 8EJ

Cartography by Philip's

Ordnance Survey® Page 2 Bath city map (top right): This product includes mapping licensed from Ordnance Survey® with the permission of the Controller of Her Majesty's Stationery Office. © Crown copyright 2003. All rights reserved. Licence number 100011710.

Illustrations by Stefan Chabluk

© 1993, 1999, 2001, 2003 Philip's
First published 1993
Second edition 1997
Third edition 1999
Fourth edition 2003

A CIP catalogue record for this book is available from the British Library.

ISBN 0–540–08311–9

Printed in Hong Kong

Details of other Philip's titles and services can be found on our website at: www.philips-maps.co.uk

What is a map?

These small maps explain the meaning of some of the lines and colours on the atlas maps.

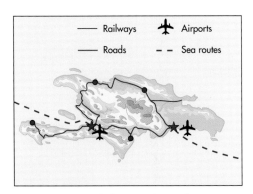

1. Land and sea This is how an island is shown on a map. The land is coloured green and the sea is blue. The coastline is a blue line.

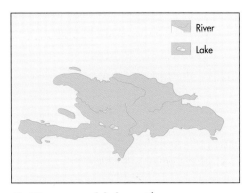

2. Rivers and lakes There are some lakes on the island and rivers that flow down to the sea.

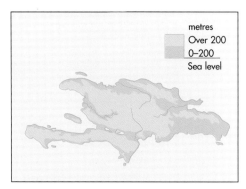

3. Height of the land – 1 This map shows the land over 200 metres high in a lighter colour. The height of the land is shown by contour lines and layer colours.

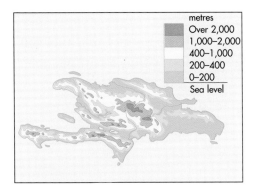

4. Height of the land – 2 This map shows more contour lines and layer colours. It shows that the highest land is in the centre of the island and that it is over 2,000 metres high.

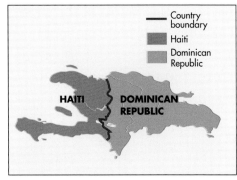

5. Countries This is a way of showing different information about the island. It shows that the island is divided into two countries. They are separated by a country boundary.

6. Cities and towns There are cities and towns on the island. The two capital cities are shown with a special symbol. Other large or important cities are also shown by a red square or circle.

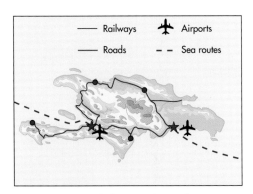

7. Transport information This map shows the most important roads, railways, airports and sea routes. Transport routes connect the cities and towns.

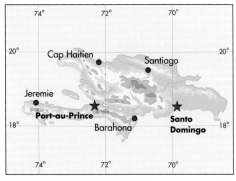

8. Where is the island? This map gives the lines of latitude and longitude and shows where the island is in the world. Page 59 in the atlas shows the same island at a different scale.

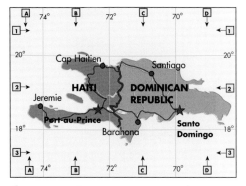

9. A complete map – using the country colouring and showing the letter-figure codes used in the index.

Scale

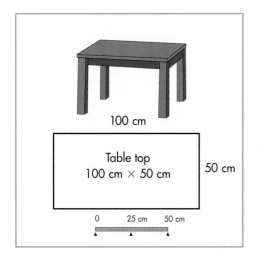

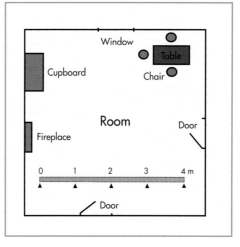

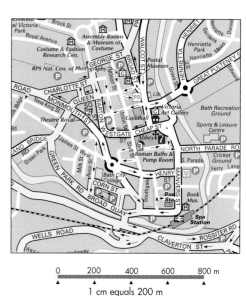

1 cm equals 200 m

This is a drawing of the top of a table, looking down on it. It is 100 cm wide and 50 cm from front to back. The drawing measures 4 × 2 cm. It is drawn to scale: 1 cm on the drawing equals 25 cm on the table.

This is a plan of a room looking down from above. 1 cm on the map equals 1 metre in the room. The same table is shown, but now at a smaller scale. Use the scale bar to find the measurements of other parts of the room.

This is a map of an area in the city of Bath. Large buildings can be seen but other buildings are too small to show. Below are atlas maps of different scales.

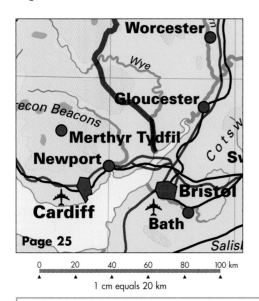

1 cm equals 20 km

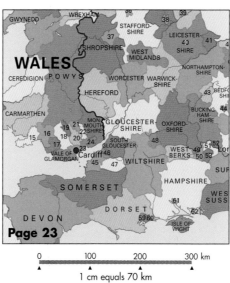

1 cm equals 70 km

1 cm equals 150 km

Scale bars
This distance represents 1 mile

This distance represents 1 kilometre

These examples of scale bars are at the scale of 1 cm equals 0.5 km

Signposts still have miles on them. 1 mile = 1.6 km, or 10 miles is the same as 16 kilometres. On maps of continents in this atlas, both a kilometre and a mile scale bar are shown.

On the maps of the continents, where you cannot see the British Isles, a small map of the British Isles is shown. It gives you some idea of size and scale.

BRITISH ISLES
On same scale

Direction

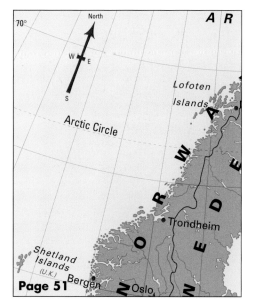

Page 51

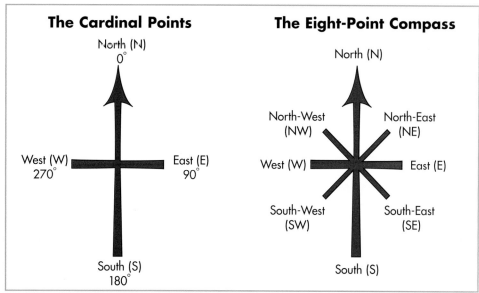

The Cardinal Points

North (N)
0°

West (W)   East (E)
270°   90°

South (S)
180°

The Eight-Point Compass

North (N)

North-West (NW)   North-East (NE)

West (W)   East (E)

South-West (SW)   South-East (SE)

South (S)

Many of the maps in this atlas have a North Point showing the direction of north. It points in the same direction as the lines of longitude. The four main directions shown are called the cardinal points.

Direction is measured in degrees. This diagram shows the degree numbers for each cardinal point. The direction is measured clockwise from north. The diagram on the right shows all the points of the compass and the divisions between the cardinal points. For example, between north and east there is north-east, between south and west is south-west. You can work out the cardinal points at your home by looking for the sun rising in the east and setting in the west.

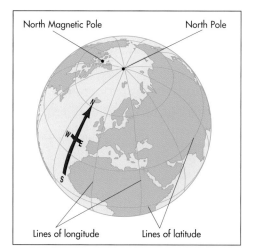

The Earth has a spot near the North Pole that is called the Magnetic Pole. If a piece of metal that was magnetized at one end was left to float, then the magnetized tip would point to the North Magnetic Pole.

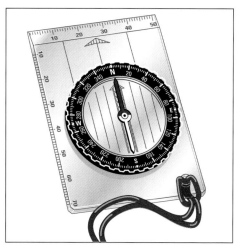

The needle of a compass is magnetized and it always points north. If you know where you are and want to go to another place, you can measure your direction from a map and use a compass to guide you.

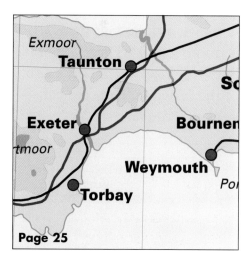

Page 25

This is part of map 25. North is at the top. Look at the points of the compass on the diagram above and the positions of places on the map. Taunton is north-east of Exeter and Weymouth is south-east of Taunton.

Latitude and longitude

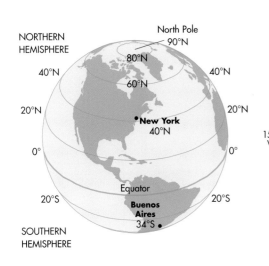

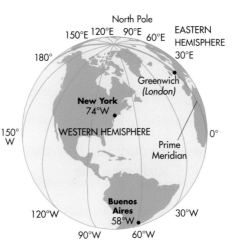

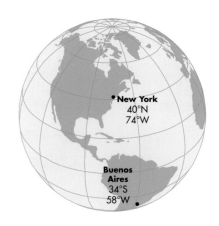

Latitude

This map shows how the Earth would look from thousands of kilometres above New York. The Equator is exactly halfway between the North and South Poles. It divides the Earth into two hemispheres. The Equator is shown as a line on maps. It is numbered 0°. There are other lines on maps north and south of the Equator. They are called lines of latitude.

Longitude

Maps have another set of lines running north to south linking the Poles. These lines are called lines of longitude. The line numbered 0° runs through Greenwich in London, England, and is called the Prime Meridian. The other lines of longitude are numbered up to 180° east and west of 0°. Longitude line 180° runs through the Pacific Ocean.

Map references

The latitude and longitude lines on maps form a grid. In this atlas, the grid lines are in blue, and on most maps are shown for every ten degrees. The numbers of the lines can be used to give a reference to show the location of a place on a map. The index in this atlas uses another way of finding places. It lists the rows of latitude as numbers and the columns of longitude as letters.

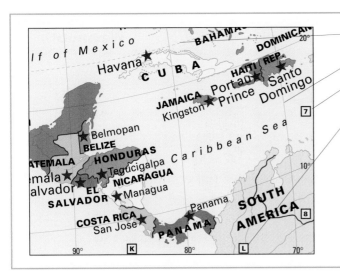

Line of latitude with its number in degrees
Line of longitude with its number in degrees
Row number used in the index
Column letter used in the index

This table shows the largest city in each continent with its latitude and longitude. Look for them on the maps in this atlas.

	Latitude	Longitude	Map page	Map letter-figure
Cairo	30°N	31°E	55	F2
Mexico City	19°N	99°W	59	H7
Moscow	56°N	38°E	51	Q4
Sao Paulo	24°S	48°W	61	F6
Shanghai	31°N	121°E	53	P5
Sydney	34°N	151°E	57	F11

Map information

Symbols

A map symbol shows the position of something – for example, circles for towns or an aeroplane for an airport.

▼

Page 17

On some maps a dot or a symbol stands for a large number – for example, ten million people or two million tonnes of wheat or potatoes.

▼
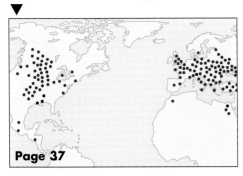
Page 37

The size of the symbol can be bigger or smaller, to show different numbers. The symbol here shows tourists.

▼
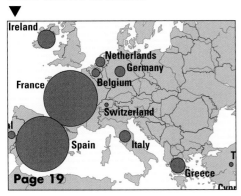
Page 19

Colours

1. Colours are used on some maps so that separate areas, such as countries, as in this map, can be seen clearly.

▼
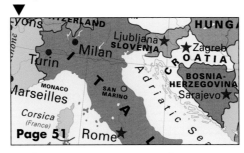
Page 51

3. Patterns on maps often spread across country borders. This map shows different types of vegetation in the world.

▼
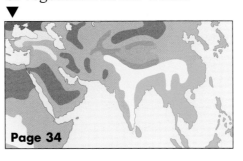
Page 34

2. On other maps, areas which are the same in some way have the same colour to show patterns. This map shows rainfall.

▼
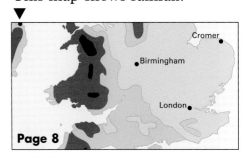
Page 8

4. Colours that are lighter or darker are used on some maps to show less or more of something. This map shows farming.

▼
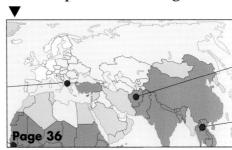
Page 36

Graphs and charts

Graphs and charts are used to give more information about subjects shown on the maps.
A graph shows how something changes over time.

This graph shows the rainfall for each month in a year as a blue bar which can be measured on the scale at the side of the graph.

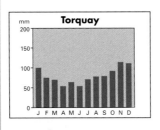
Page 8

This diagram is called a pie-chart. It shows how you can divide a total into its parts.

Page 15

This is a bar-chart. It is another way of showing a total divided into parts.

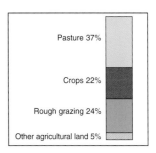
Page 13

— Rocks, mountains and rivers —

Rocks

This map shows the different types of rock in Great Britain and Ireland.

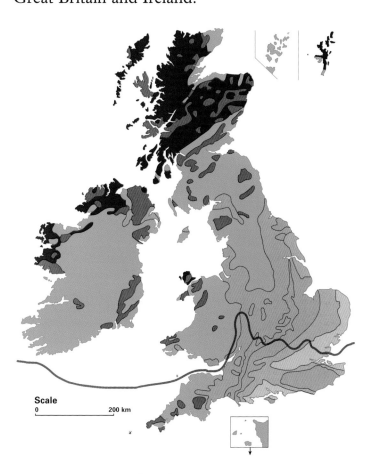

Scale
0   200 km

Type of rock

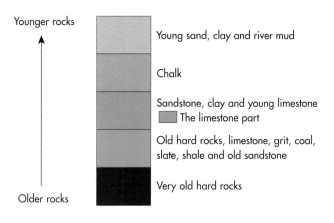

Younger rocks ↑

Young sand, clay and river mud

Chalk

Sandstone, clay and young limestone
☐ The limestone part

Old hard rocks, limestone, grit, coal, slate, shale and old sandstone

Very old hard rocks

Older rocks

Old volcanoes, granite and basalt

Glaciers came as far south as this line up to 10,000 years ago

---

Longest rivers
(length in kilometres)

Shannon	370
Severn	354
Thames	335
Trent	297
Aire	259
Ouse	230
Wye	215
Tay	188
Nene	161
Clyde	158

Largest islands
(square kilometres)

Great Britain	229,880
Ireland	84,400
Lewis and Harris	2,225
Skye	1,666
Shetland (Mainland)	967
Mull	899
Anglesey	714
Islay	615
Isle of Man	572
Isle of Wight	381

Largest lakes
(square kilometres)

Lough Neagh	382
Lough Corrib	168
Lough Derg	120
Lower Lough Erne	105
Loch Lomond	71
Loch Ness	57

The largest lake in England is Lake Windermere (15 square kilometres). The largest lake in Wales is Lake Vyrnwy (8 square kilometres).

Highest mountains
(height in metres)

In Scotland:
  Ben Nevis 1,347
In Wales:
  Snowdon 1,085
In Ireland:
  Carrauntoohill 1,041
In England:
  Scafell Pike 978
In Northern Ireland:
  Slieve Donard 852

Scale
0   200 km

6

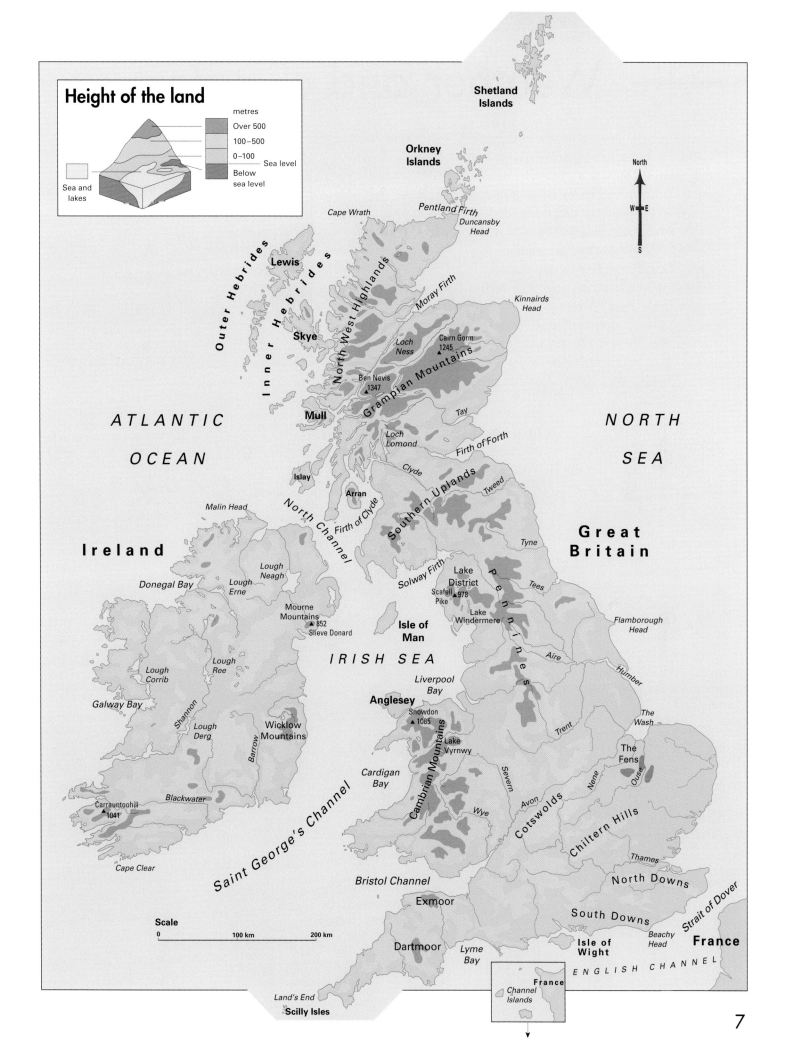

Height of the land

metres

Over 500

100–500

0–100 — Sea level

Below sea level

Sea and lakes

North

W — E

S

Shetland Islands

Orkney Islands

Cape Wrath

Pentland Firth

Duncansby Head

Outer Hebrides

Lewis

Inner Hebrides

Skye

North West Highlands

Moray Firth

Kinnairds Head

Loch Ness

Cairn Gorm 1245

Grampian Mountains

Ben Nevis 1347

Mull

Tay

ATLANTIC OCEAN

Loch Lomond

Islay

Firth of Forth

Clyde

Arran

Firth of Clyde

Southern Uplands

Tweed

NORTH SEA

Malin Head

North Channel

Tyne

Ireland

Great Britain

Donegal Bay

Lough Neagh

Lough Erne

Solway Firth

Lake District

Tees

Scafell Pike 978

Pennines

Mourne Mountains 852

Lake Windermere

Flamborough Head

Slieve Donard

Isle of Man

Lough Corrib

Lough Ree

IRISH SEA

Aire

Humber

Galway Bay

Shannon

Lough Derg

Wicklow Mountains

Barrow

Liverpool Bay

Anglesey

Snowdon 1085

Trent

The Wash

Carrauntoohill 1041

Blackwater

Cardigan Bay

Cambrian Mountains

Lake Vyrnwy

The Fens

Ouse

Nene

Chiltern Hills

Severn

Avon

Cotswolds

Cape Clear

Saint George's Channel

Wye

Thames

North Downs

Scale

0   100 km   200 km

Bristol Channel

Exmoor

South Downs

Beachy Head

Strait of Dover

Isle of Wight

France

Dartmoor

Lyme Bay

ENGLISH CHANNEL

Land's End

Scilly Isles

France

Channel Islands

7

Weather and climate

Rainfall is measured at many places in the UK every day. Each year, all the measurements are put together and graphs are made, like the ones shown on this page. Experts in the weather use these measurements to find out the average amount of rainfall in the UK for each year. They can then show this on weather maps, like the map below. Graphs and maps are also made for average temperatures and other types of weather (see opposite page). These help the experts to see patterns in the UK's weather over a long period of time. These patterns in the weather show a country's climate. The maps on these pages show you the climate of the UK.

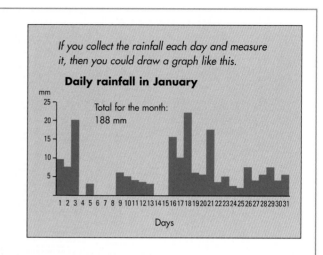

If you collect the rainfall each day and measure it, then you could draw a graph like this.

Daily rainfall in January

Total for the month: 188 mm

Rainfall

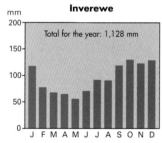

Inverewe — Total for the year: 1,128 mm

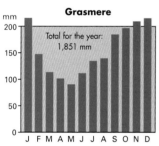

Grasmere — Total for the year: 1,851 mm

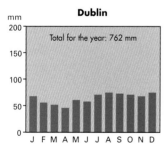

Dublin — Total for the year: 762 mm

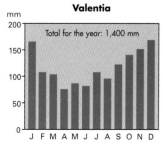

Valentia — Total for the year: 1,400 mm

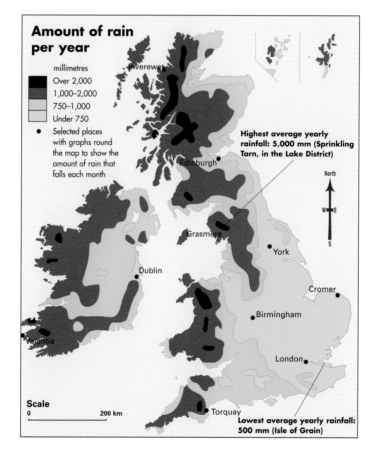

Amount of rain per year

millimetres
- Over 2,000
- 1,000–2,000
- 750–1,000
- Under 750
- Selected places with graphs round the map to show the amount of rain that falls each month

Highest average yearly rainfall: 5,000 mm (Sprinkling Tarn, in the Lake District)

North
W E
S

Lowest average yearly rainfall: 500 mm (Isle of Grain)

Scale
0   200 km

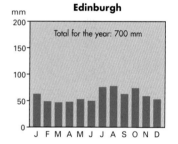

Edinburgh — Total for the year: 700 mm

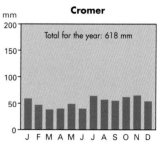

York — Total for the year: 639 mm

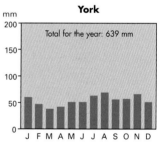

Cromer — Total for the year: 618 mm

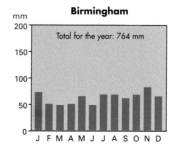

Torquay — Total for the year: 950 mm

Birmingham — Total for the year: 764 mm

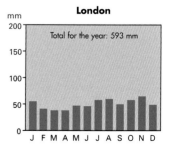

London — Total for the year: 593 mm

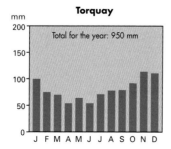

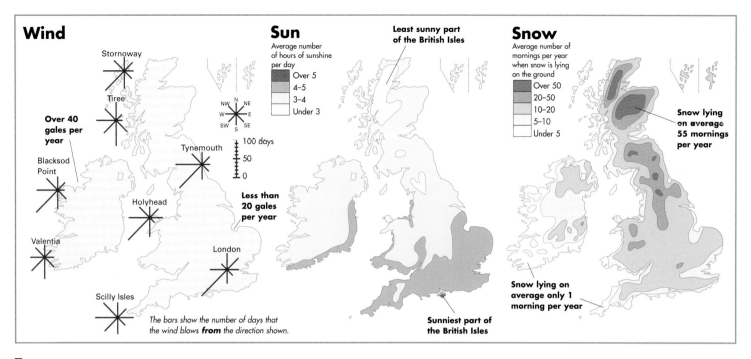

Wind

Stornoway

Tiree

Over 40 gales per year

Blacksod Point

Tynemouth

Holyhead

Valentia

London

Scilly Isles

Less than 20 gales per year

*The bars show the number of days that the wind blows **from** the direction shown.*

100 days
50
0

Sun

Average number of hours of sunshine per day

Over 5
4–5
3–4
Under 3

Least sunny part of the British Isles

Sunniest part of the British Isles

Snow

Average number of mornings per year when snow is lying on the ground

Over 50
20–50
10–20
5–10
Under 5

Snow lying on average 55 mornings per year

Snow lying on average only 1 morning per year

Temperature

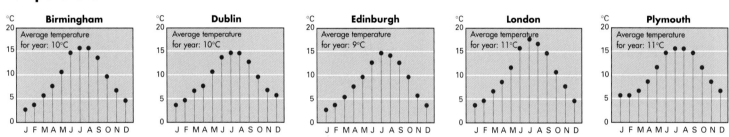

Birmingham — Average temperature for year: 10°C

Dublin — Average temperature for year: 10°C

Edinburgh — Average temperature for year: 9°C

London — Average temperature for year: 11°C

Plymouth — Average temperature for year: 11°C

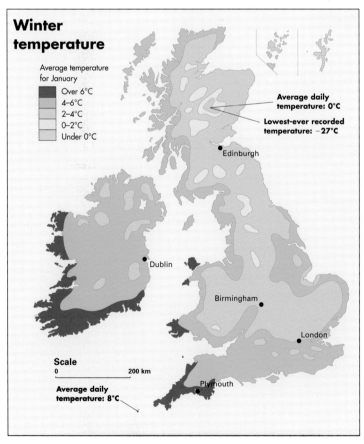

Winter temperature

Average temperature for January

Over 6°C
4–6°C
2–4°C
0–2°C
Under 0°C

Average daily temperature: 0°C

Lowest-ever recorded temperature: –27°C

Edinburgh

Dublin

Birmingham

London

Plymouth

Scale
0   200 km

Average daily temperature: 8°C

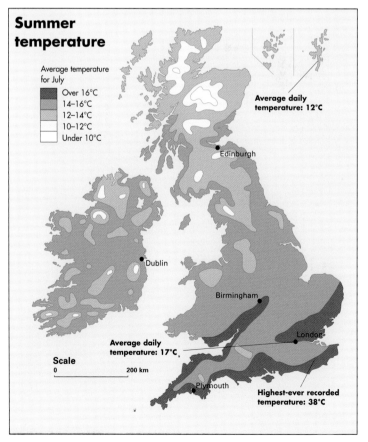

Summer temperature

Average temperature for July

Over 16°C
14–16°C
12–14°C
10–12°C
Under 10°C

Average daily temperature: 12°C

Edinburgh

Dublin

Birmingham

London

Plymouth

Average daily temperature: 17°C

Highest-ever recorded temperature: 38°C

Scale
0   200 km

9

People, cities and towns

The Census

Every ten years, there is a government survey in the UK. The head of each household has to fill in a form. On the form, there are questions about the house and the people who live there. This is called the Census. The Census tells the government the number of people living in the UK. This helps the government to plan such things as schools and hospitals. The Census shows how the population has changed during the last century.

Here are some of the questions asked on the Census form:
Age?
Have you moved house in the last year?
In which country were you born?
To which ethnic group do you belong?
Have you a long-term illness?
Can you speak Welsh?
What do you do for a job?
How many hours a week do you work?
How do you get to work?
Where do you work?
Do you own or rent your house?
Do you have a bath, flush toilet or central heating?
Do you have a car?

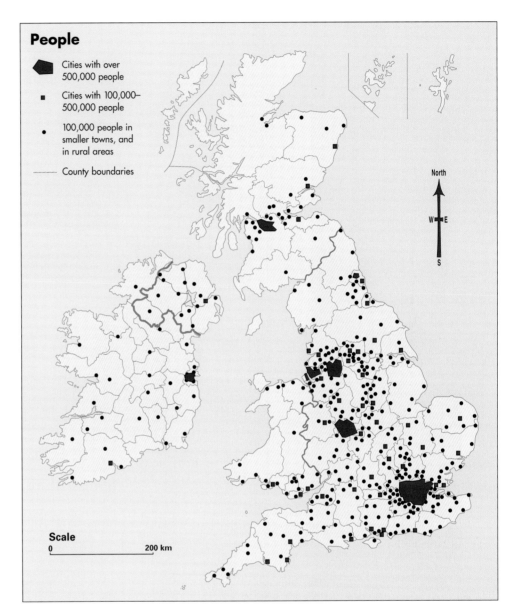

People

- Cities with over 500,000 people
- Cities with 100,000–500,000 people
- 100,000 people in smaller towns, and in rural areas
- County boundaries

Scale
0 — 200 km

Country population data

	1901	1951	2001
		millions	
England	30.5	41.2	49.2
Wales	2.0	2.6	2.9
Scotland	4.5	5.1	5.1
Northern Ireland	1.2	1.4	1.7
United Kingdom	**38.2**	**50.3**	**58.9**
Isle of Man	0.055	0.005	0.076
Channel Islands	0.096	0.102	0.147
Ireland	**3.2**	**2.9**	**3.9**

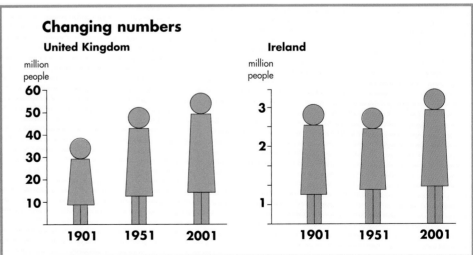

Changing numbers

United Kingdom — million people — 1901 1951 2001

Ireland — million people — 1901 1951 2001

Cities

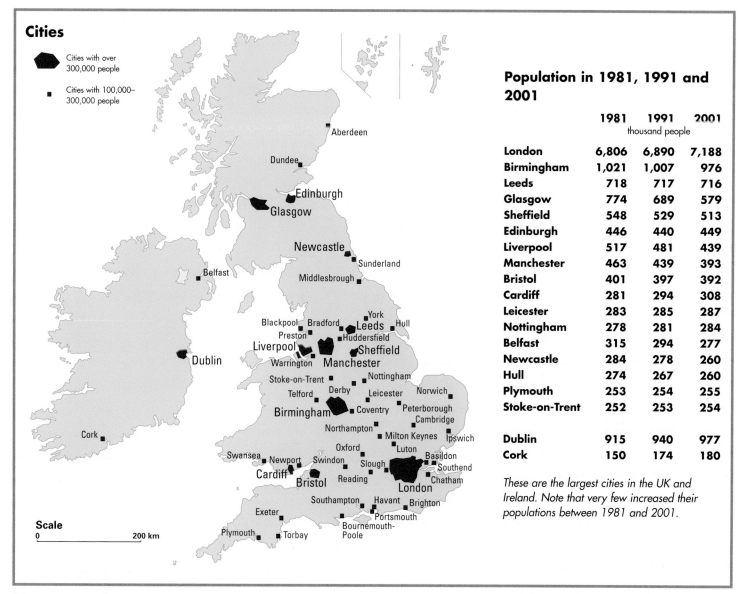

Cities

◆ Cities with over 300,000 people

▪ Cities with 100,000–300,000 people

Scale
0 — 200 km

Population in 1981, 1991 and 2001

	1981	1991	2001
	thousand people		
London	6,806	6,890	7,188
Birmingham	1,021	1,007	976
Leeds	718	717	716
Glasgow	774	689	579
Sheffield	548	529	513
Edinburgh	446	440	449
Liverpool	517	481	439
Manchester	463	439	393
Bristol	401	397	392
Cardiff	281	294	308
Leicester	283	285	287
Nottingham	278	281	284
Belfast	315	294	277
Newcastle	284	278	260
Hull	274	267	260
Plymouth	253	254	255
Stoke-on-Trent	252	253	254
Dublin	915	940	977
Cork	150	174	180

These are the largest cities in the UK and Ireland. Note that very few increased their populations between 1981 and 2001.

Young people

In these counties, young people are a large group in the population (over 20%). On this map young people are those aged under 15 years old.

In these counties, old people are a large group in the population (over 20%). On this map old people are women aged over 60 and men over 65 years old.

Look at these two maps. Can you think of some reasons why some counties have more older people than other counties?

Old people

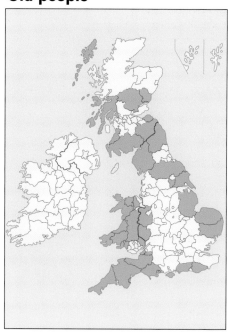

Farming and fishing

Types of farm

Dairy farms
Cows for milk, butter and cheese

Beef farms
Cows and calves for beef and veal

Sheep farms
Sheep and lambs for wool and meat

Grain and root farms
Wheat, potatoes, sugar beet and oilseed rape

Mixed farms
Livestock and grain or roots

Market gardening
Vegetables, fruit and flowers

Forests

Big cities

The small maps show where different types of crops are grown.

North
W E
S

Scale
0   200 km

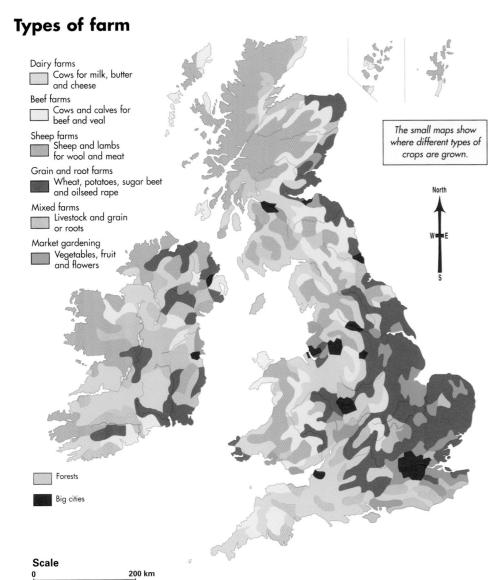

Wheat

square kilometres
Over 1,000

250–1,000 in each county

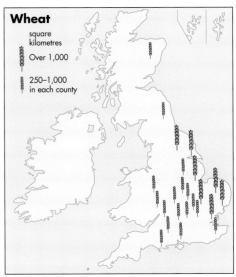

Potatoes

square kilometres
Over 100

25–100 in each county

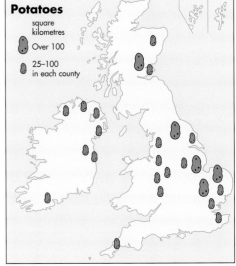

Oilseed rape

square kilometres
Over 200

50–200 in each county

Sugar beet

square kilometres
Over 100

10–100 in each county

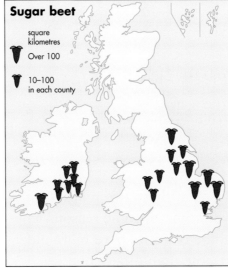

Vegetables

square kilometres
Over 100

10–100 in each county

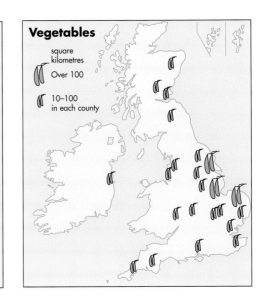

Cattle

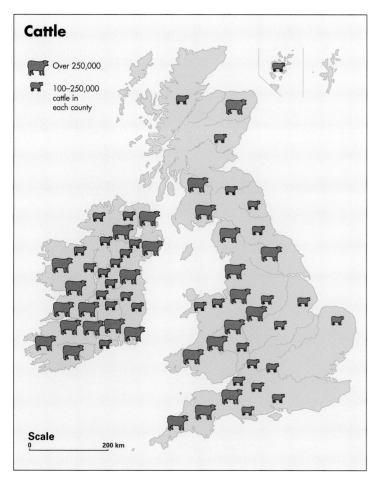

Over 250,000

100–250,000 cattle in each county

Scale
0   200 km

Sheep and pigs

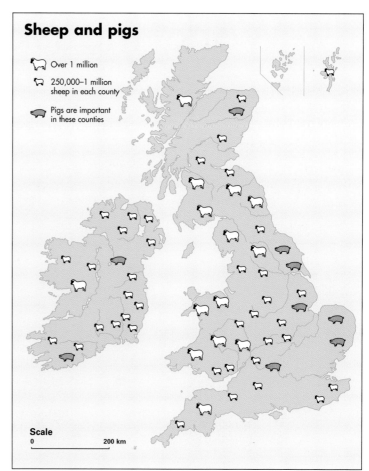

Over 1 million

250,000–1 million sheep in each county

Pigs are important in these counties

Scale
0   200 km

Land use in the UK

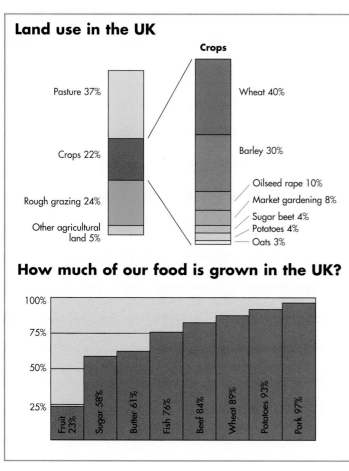

Crops

Pasture 37%

Crops 22%

Rough grazing 24%

Other agricultural land 5%

Wheat 40%

Barley 30%

Oilseed rape 10%
Market gardening 8%
Sugar beet 4%
Potatoes 4%
Oats 3%

How much of our food is grown in the UK?

100%
75%
50%
25%

Fruit 23%
Sugar 58%
Butter 61%
Fish 76%
Beef 84%
Wheat 89%
Potatoes 93%
Pork 97%

Fishing

Large fishing ports (over 50,000 tonnes of fish caught each year)

Small fishing ports

Ullapool
Fraserburgh
Peterhead
Aberdeen

Greencastle
Ayr
North Shields
Killybegs
Whitby
Scarborough
Bridlington
Fleetwood
Hull
Grimsby

Rossaveel
Howth
Lowestoft

Castletownbere
Cobh
Dunmore East
Milford Haven

Plymouth
Brixham
Falmouth
Newlyn

Scale
0   200 km

13

— Work, industry and energy —

Manufacturing

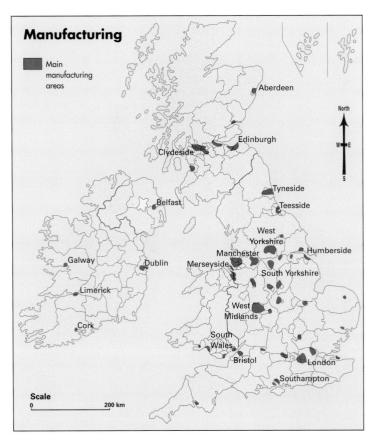

■ Main manufacturing areas

Aberdeen
Edinburgh
Clydeside
Tyneside
Belfast
Teesside
West Yorkshire
Galway
Manchester
Humberside
Merseyside
Dublin
South Yorkshire
Limerick
West Midlands
Cork
South Wales
Bristol
London
Southampton

North
W — E
S

Scale
0 ——— 200 km

Manufacturing industries are industries which make things. Some examples of manufactured goods are cars, steel, textiles and clothes.

Unemployment

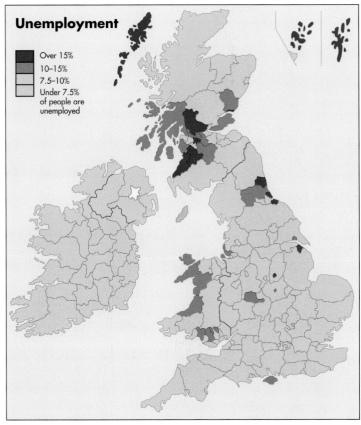

■ Over 15%
■ 10–15%
■ 7.5–10%
□ Under 7.5% of people are unemployed

Service industries do not make things. They provide a service to people. Shops, hotels and banks are examples of service industries.

Employment in manufacturing

■ Over 25% of people who work are employed in manufacturing industries

Employment in services

■ Over 70% of people who work are employed in the service industries

Employment in agriculture

% of people who work are employed in agriculture, forestry or fishing

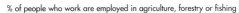

□ 2.5–10%   ■ Over 10%

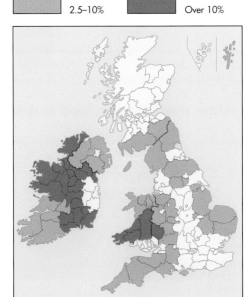

Sources of energy used in the United Kingdom

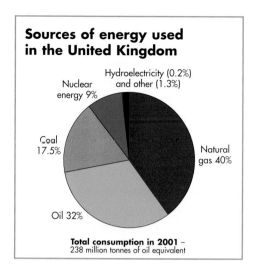

Nuclear energy 9%

Hydroelectricity (0.2%) and other (1.3%)

Coal 17.5%

Oil 32%

Natural gas 40%

Total consumption in 2001 –
238 million tonnes of oil equivalent

Electricity generation in the United Kingdom (1980–2000)

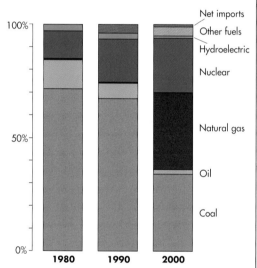

Net imports
Other fuels
Hydroelectric
Nuclear
Natural gas
Oil
Coal

100%

50%

0%

1980 1990 2000

This bar-chart shows the different types of fuel that are used to make electricity in the UK. The use of coal in the generation of electricity has dropped over the 20-year period from 1980 to 2000. However, the use of nuclear power has increased by 58%.

Coal mining and miners in the UK (1950–2000)

	1950	1970	2000
Number of miners (in thousands)	686	356	13
Number of mines	901	292	18
Coal produced (million tonnes)	220	145	17

You can see from the table that there were less mines and miners in 2000 than 1950. Britain's pits and open-cast mines were sold by the government on 30 December 1994 (ending 48 years of state ownership). The new owners paid almost £1,000 million to the government for the mines and coal reserves. There are thought to be 700 million tonnes of coal left in the ground.

Energy sources in Great Britain and Ireland

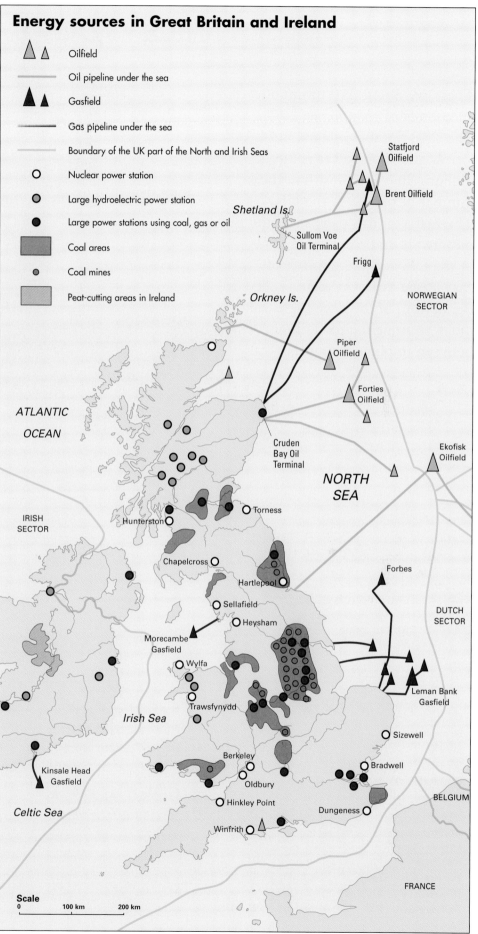

Oilfield

Oil pipeline under the sea

Gasfield

Gas pipeline under the sea

Boundary of the UK part of the North and Irish Seas

Nuclear power station

Large hydroelectric power station

Large power stations using coal, gas or oil

Coal areas

Coal mines

Peat-cutting areas in Ireland

Transport

There are about 370 thousand kilometres of road in the UK. The total number of cars, buses, lorries and motorbikes is 26 million. That is almost half the number of people in the UK. The maps on this page show the motorways and some main roads in the UK and the number of cars in the different regions. At the bottom of the page there are tables showing the road distances between important towns.

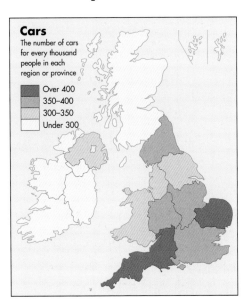

Cars
The number of cars for every thousand people in each region or province

- Over 400
- 350–400
- 300–350
- Under 300

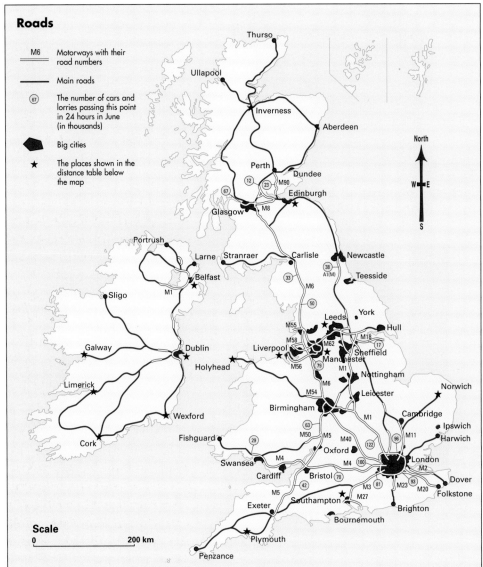

Roads

M6	Motorways with their road numbers
—	Main roads
⓺⑦	The number of cars and lorries passing this point in 24 hours in June (in thousands)
◆	Big cities
★	The places shown in the distance table below the map

North
W—E
S

Scale
0 ————— 200 km

Road distances

The distance tables are in kilometres, but distances on road signposts in the UK are in miles.
A mile is longer than a kilometre.
1 mile = 1.6 kilometres. 1 kilometre = 0.6 mile.

UK	Birmingham	Cardiff	Edinburgh	Holyhead	Inverness	Leeds	Liverpool	London	Manchester	Norwich	Plymouth	Southampton
Birmingham		163	460	246	716	179	151	179	130	249	320	206
Cardiff	163		587	341	843	341	264	249	277	381	259	192
Edinburgh	460	587		489	256	320	338	608	336	586	790	669
Holyhead	246	341	489		745	262	151	420	198	481	528	455
Inverness	716	843	256	745		579	605	864	604	842	1049	925
Leeds	179	341	320	262	579		119	306	64	277	502	378
Liverpool	151	264	338	151	605	119		330	55	360	452	357
London	179	249	608	420	864	306	330		309	172	343	127
Manchester	130	277	336	198	604	64	55	309		306	457	325
Norwich	249	381	586	481	842	277	360	172	306		515	299
Plymouth	320	259	790	528	1049	502	452	343	457	515		246
Southampton	206	192	669	455	925	378	357	127	325	299	246	

Ireland

	Belfast	Cork	Dublin	Galway	Limerick	Wexford
Belfast		418	160	300	222	306
Cork	418		257	193	97	190
Dublin	160	257		210	193	137
Galway	300	193	210		97	249
Limerick	222	97	193	97		193
Wexford	306	190	137	249	193	

Railways

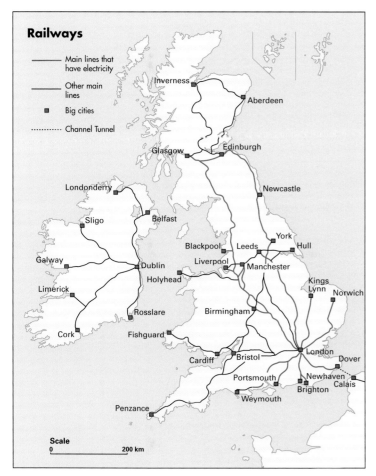

- Main lines that have electricity
- Other main lines
- Big cities
- Channel Tunnel

Inverness · Aberdeen · Glasgow · Edinburgh · Londonderry · Sligo · Belfast · Newcastle · Galway · Dublin · Blackpool · Leeds · York · Hull · Liverpool · Manchester · Holyhead · Limerick · Kings Lynn · Norwich · Rosslare · Birmingham · Cork · Fishguard · Cardiff · Bristol · London · Dover · Portsmouth · Newhaven · Calais · Weymouth · Brighton · Penzance

Scale
0   200 km

Manchester – the daily flow of people

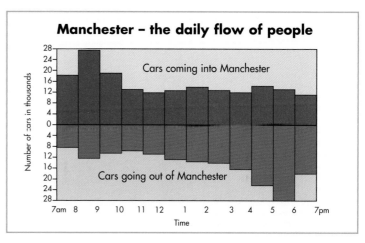

Number of cars in thousands

Cars coming into Manchester

Cars going out of Manchester

7am 8 9 10 11 12 1 2 3 4 5 6 7pm
Time

The Channel Tunnel

Edinburgh · Holyhead · Copenhage · Channel Tunnel · Cardiff · Hamburg · London · Brussels · Berlin · Dover · Calais · Frankfurt · Rennes · Paris · Munich · Bordeaux · Lyons · Berne · Milan · Bilbao · Marseilles · Madrid · Barcelona · Naples

The Channel Tunnel is 50 kilometres long and trains run through it in just 21 minutes.

Journey time to Paris by train

from	Today	Year 2010
	hours and minutes	
London	3.00	2.30
Birmingham	6.30	4.15
Manchester	8.15	5.15
Newcastle	8.30	6.00
Edinburgh	10.00	7.30

By the year 2010 trains will be able to travel at over 250 km/h on those lines shown on the map.

Ports and ferries

- Major ports
- Other ports
- These ports are handling mainly fuel
- Important canals and rivers carrying goods
- Ferries

Orkney Is. · Sullom Voe · Ullapool · Cromarty Firth · Orkney · Peterhead · Shetland Is. · Aberdeen · Dundee · Glensanda · Oban · Clyde · Forth · Ayr · Cairnryan · Blyth · Norway, Sweden, Denmark · Larne · Stranraer · Tyne · Sunderland · Belfast · Tees and Hartlepool · Sligo · Heysham · Warrenpoint · Fleetwood · Aire & Calder · Hull · Drogheda · Liverpool · Goole · Netherlands, Belgium · Dublin · Manchester · Boston · Grimsby and Immingham · Holyhead · Manchester Ship Canal · River Trent · Great Yarmouth · Limerick · New Ross · Kings Lynn · River Yare · Foynes · Waterford · Rosslare · Felixstowe · Bantry Bay · Cork · Fishguard · River Severn · Ipswich · Harwich · Neth. Belg. · Swansea · Newport · River Thames · Milford Haven · Port Talbot · Cardiff · Bristol · London · Medway · Ramsgate · Southampton · Shoreham · Folkestone · Dover · France · Poole · Portsmouth · Newhaven · Fowey · Plymouth · France · Channel Is. · France · Caledonian Canal · Spain · Scilly Isles

Scale
0   200 km

Airports

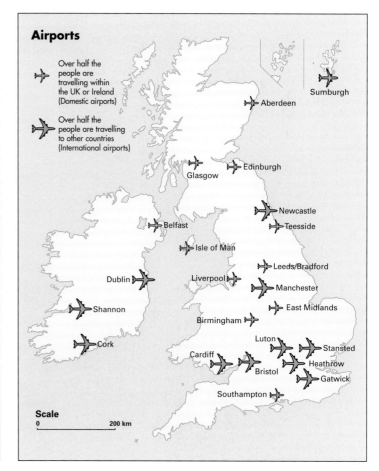

- Over half the people are travelling within the UK or Ireland (Domestic airports)
- Over half the people are travelling to other countries (International airports)

Sumburgh · Aberdeen · Glasgow · Edinburgh · Belfast · Newcastle · Teesside · Isle of Man · Leeds/Bradford · Dublin · Liverpool · Manchester · Shannon · Birmingham · East Midlands · Luton · Stansted · Cork · Cardiff · Heathrow · Bristol · Gatwick · Southampton

Scale
0   200 km

Tourism and conservation

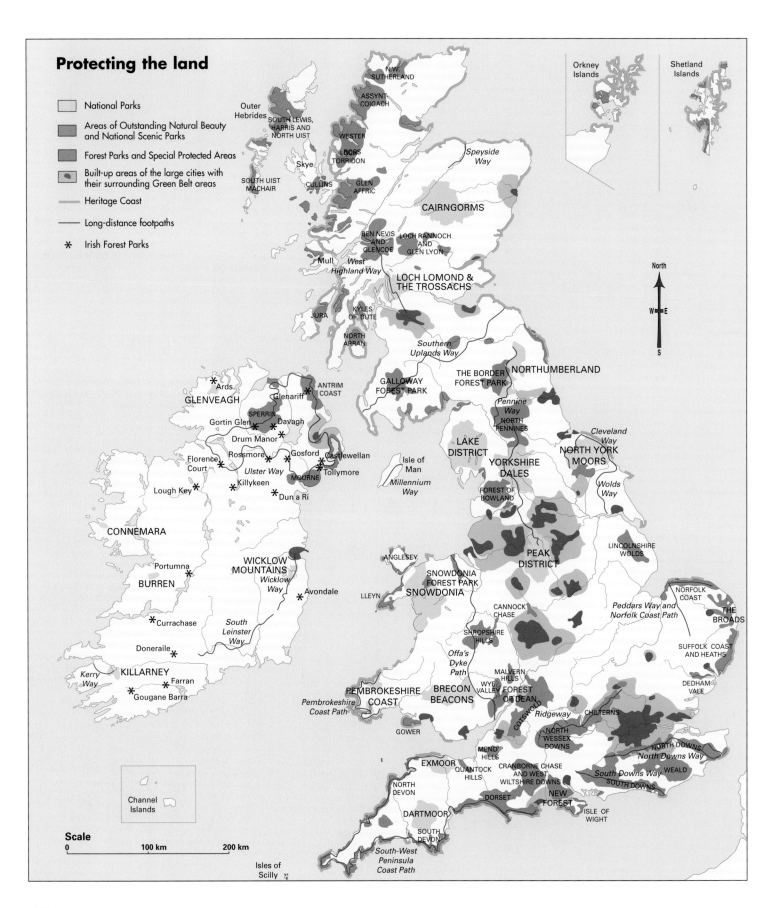

Protecting the land

- National Parks
- Areas of Outstanding Natural Beauty and National Scenic Parks
- Forest Parks and Special Protected Areas
- Built-up areas of the large cities with their surrounding Green Belt areas
- Heritage Coast
- Long-distance footpaths
- ✻ Irish Forest Parks

Orkney Islands

Shetland Islands

N.W. SUTHERLAND

ASSYNT-COIGACH

Outer Hebrides

SOUTH LEWIS, HARRIS AND NORTH UIST

WESTER LOOKS

Speyside Way

Skye

TORRIDON

SOUTH UIST MACHAIR

CULLINS

GLEN AFFRIC

CAIRNGORMS

North

W E

S

BEN NEVIS AND GLENCOE

LOCH RANNOCH AND GLEN LYON

Mull

West Highland Way

LOCH LOMOND & THE TROSSACHS

JURA

KYLES OF BUTE

Southern Uplands Way

NORTH ARRAN

GALLOWAY FOREST PARK

THE BORDER FOREST PARK

NORTHUMBERLAND

✻ Ards

✻ ANTRIM COAST

GLENVEAGH

Glenariff

SPERRIN

Gortin Glen ✻

Davagh ✻

Drum Manor ✻

Pennine Way

NORTH PENNINES

Rossmore ✻

Gosford ✻ Castlewellan

LAKE DISTRICT

Cleveland Way

NORTH YORK MOORS

Florence Court ✻

Ulster Way

Killeen ✻

MOURNE

Tollymore

YORKSHIRE DALES

Wolds Way

Lough Key ✻

✻ Dun a Ri

Isle of Man

Millennium Way

FOREST OF BOWLAND

CONNEMARA

WICKLOW MOUNTAINS

ANGLESEY

PEAK DISTRICT

LINCOLNSHIRE WOLDS

Portumna ✻

Wicklow Way

SNOWDONIA FOREST PARK

BURREN

✻ Avondale

LLEYN

SNOWDONIA

CANNOCK CHASE

NORFOLK COAST

THE BROADS

✻ Currachase

South Leinster Way

SHROPSHIRE HILLS

Peddars Way and Norfolk Coast Path

Doneraile ✻

Offa's Dyke Path

MALVERN HILLS

SUFFOLK COAST AND HEATHS

KILLARNEY

✻ Farran

PEMBROKESHIRE COAST

WYE VALLEY

BRECON BEACONS

FOREST OF DEAN

DEDHAM VALE

Kerry Way

✻ Gougane Barra

Pembrokeshire Coast Path

COTSWOLD

Ridgeway

CHILTERNS

NORTH WESSEX DOWNS

NORTH DOWNS/ *North Downs Way*

GOWER

MENDIP HILLS

CRANBORNE CHASE AND WEST WILTSHIRE DOWNS

South Downs Way

WEALD

SOUTH DOWNS

EXMOOR

QUANTOCK HILLS

NEW FOREST

NORTH DEVON

DORSET

ISLE OF WIGHT

DARTMOOR

SOUTH DEVON

Channel Islands

Scale

0   100 km   200 km

South-West Peninsula Coast Path

Isles of Scilly

Holidays abroad by means of travel

thousands

Legend:
- Tunnel
- Sea
- Air

This shows the number of visits taken by people who live in Great Britain.

British tourists to other countries (2001)

(number of tourists in thousands)

Country	Number
France	11,959
Spain	11,790
USA	3,990
Ireland	3,930
Greece	3,215
Italy	2,471
Germany	2,242
Netherlands	2,095
Belgium	1,738
Portugal	1,598
Cyprus	1,476
Turkey	878
Switzerland	792
Canada	666

10 million visitors from UK
7.5 million
5 million
2.5 million
1 million

Tourism

- Main holiday cities and towns
- Major tourist attractions

Scale
0 —————— 200 km

Visitors from other countries (2001)

(number of visitors in thousands)

Country	Number
USA	3,580
France	2,852
Germany	2,309
Ireland	2,039
Netherlands	1,411
Belgium	916
Italy	857
Spain	856
Australia	694
Canada	647
Sweden	527
Switzerland	514
Norway	403

Tourist attractions (2001)

(number of visitors in millions)

Blackpool Pleasure Beach	6.5
National Gallery, London	4.9
British Museum, London	4.8
British Airways London Eye	3.9
Tate Modern, London	3.6
Alton Towers, Staffordshire	2.5
Adventure Island, Southend	2.5
Madame Tussaud's Waxworks, London	2.4
Pleasureland, Southport	2.1
Tower of London	2.0
York Minster	1.8
Clacton Pier	1.8
Eden Project, St Austell	1.7
Natural History Museum, London	1.7
Legoland, Windsor	1.6
Great Yarmouth Pleasure Beach	1.5
Chessington World of Adventures	1.5
Science Museum, London	1.4
Victoria and Albert Museum, London	1.4
Flamingo Land, Kirby Misperton	1.3

Water

Rainfall areas – wet and dry

The wet west
Monthly rainfall graph for Grasmere

mm
Year – 1,851 mm

J F M A M J J A S O N D

The dry east
Monthly rainfall graph for Cambridge

mm
Year – 558 mm

J F M A M J J A S O N D

In these areas a lot of rain (over 1,000 mm) falls nearly every year

In these areas less than 1,000 mm of rain falls

Scale
0   200 km

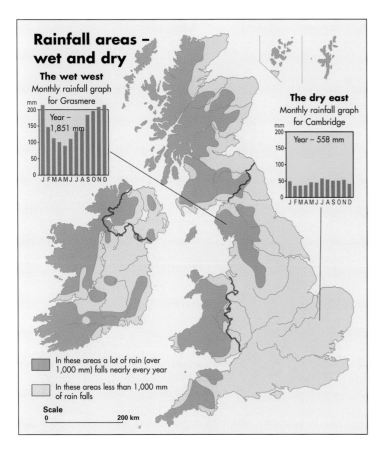

Reservoirs and boreholes

Big reservoirs

Areas where water is got out of the ground with boreholes

The water flows to where it is used, either along rivers or through pipelines

The big cities where a lot of water is needed

North
W E
S

Loch Lomond
Loch Katrine
Kielder Res.
Thirlmere
Cow Green Res.
Haweswater
Pollaphuca Res.
Elan Valley
Rutland Water
Grafham Water

Scale
0   200 km

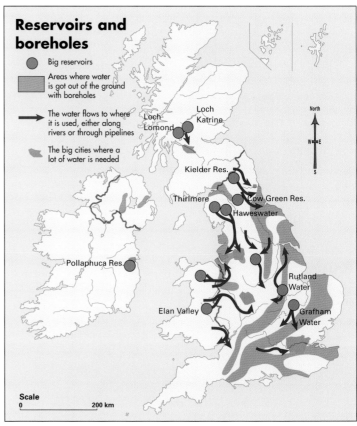

River pollution

Badly polluted rivers

Over 15%

10% – 15%

5% – 10%

Under 5%
of the rivers in these areas are of poor or bad quality

No information for Ireland

Sea areas where sewage and other waste is dumped

Scale
0   200 km

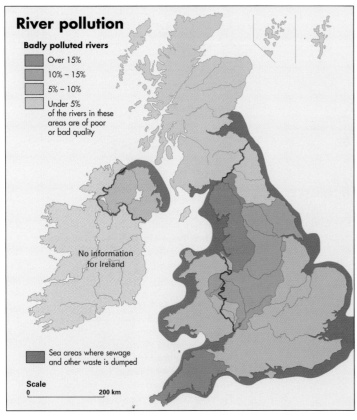

Water supply

THAMES   Environment Agency Region

2754   Water supply in megalitres per day (domestic use, not for industry or agriculture)

SCOTLAND
2400

N. IRELAND
720

NORTH EAST
2024

NORTH WEST
2016

No data

MIDLANDS
2198

ANGLIAN
2566

WELSH
1093

THAMES
2754

SOUTH WEST
1260

SOUTHERN
1349

Scale
0   200 km

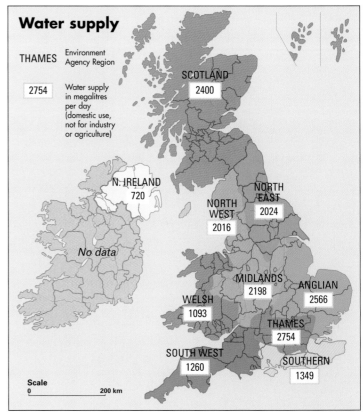

Water use in the United Kingdom

The average UK household uses 355 litres of water a day.
Up to 135,000 million litres of water are used each day in the UK.
Over half the water is used by people in their homes. About a third is used to make electricity. The rest is used in farms and factories. On the right are some of the ways that water is used in the home:

To make one car can use up to 30,000 litres of water. To brew one pint of beer needs 8 pints of water.

Domestic appliances – water usage

	(per wash)
Washing machine	80 litres
Bath	80 litres
Dishwasher	35 litres
Shower	35 litres
Toilet flush	10 litres

The water cycle

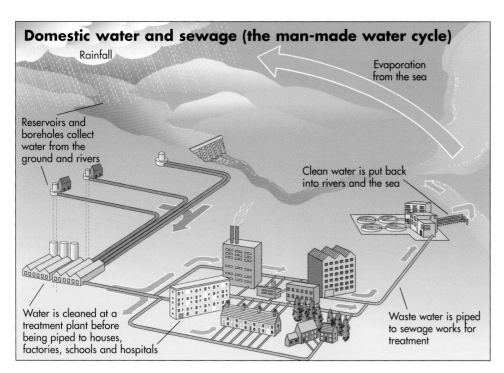

Domestic water and sewage (the man-made water cycle)

Acid rain in Britain

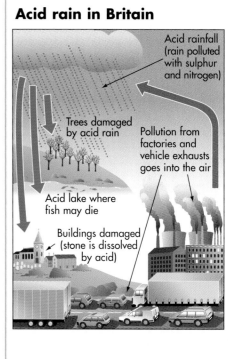

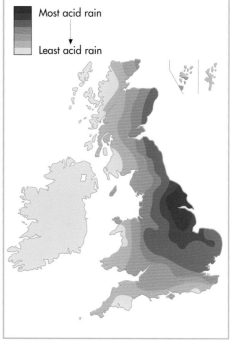

21

Counties and regions

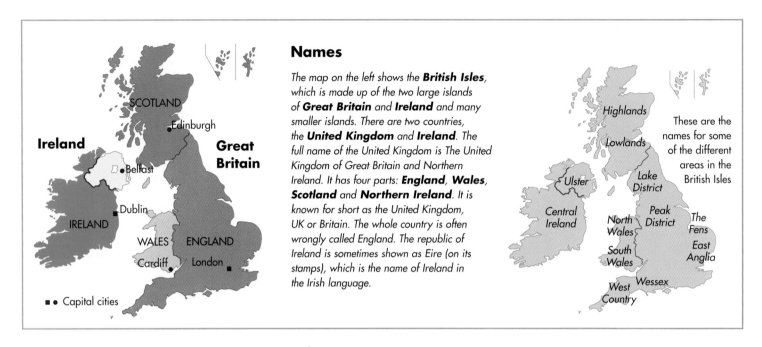

Names

The map on the left shows the **British Isles**, which is made up of the two large islands of **Great Britain** and **Ireland** and many smaller islands. There are two countries, the **United Kingdom** and **Ireland**. The full name of the United Kingdom is The United Kingdom of Great Britain and Northern Ireland. It has four parts: **England**, **Wales**, **Scotland** and **Northern Ireland**. It is known for short as the United Kingdom, UK or Britain. The whole country is often wrongly called England. The republic of Ireland is sometimes shown as Eire (on its stamps), which is the name of Ireland in the Irish language.

These are the names for some of the different areas in the British Isles

Counties and regions

The map shows the Standard Regions of the United Kingdom. The boundaries follow those of the counties shown on page 23. Large bodies like the Health Service, Water or Electricity divide the country up into their own regions. Ireland is divided into four historic provinces.

Counties and unitary authorities

England and Wales are divided into counties, unitary authorities and boroughs. The counties are divided into districts, and the districts into parishes and wards. Scotland is divided into regions and unitary authorities, and Northern Ireland into districts.

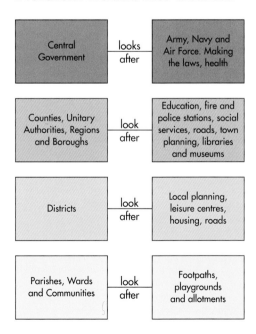

Central Government	looks after	Army, Navy and Air Force. Making the laws, health
Counties, Unitary Authorities, Regions and Boroughs	look after	Education, fire and police stations, social services, roads, town planning, libraries and museums
Districts	look after	Local planning, leisure centres, housing, roads
Parishes, Wards and Communities	look after	Footpaths, playgrounds and allotments

Area data

	Area in square kilometres
England	130,439
Wales	20,768
Scotland	77,167
Northern Ireland	13,483
United Kingdom	**241,857**
Isle of Man	**572**
Channel Islands	**195**
Ireland	**68,896**

The Channel Islands and the Isle of Man are dependencies of the Crown and have their own parliaments. They are not part of the United Kingdom.

The six counties are shown in Northern Ireland. It is divided for local government into 26 districts.

The map shows the 6 counties in Northern Ireland, the 32 unitary authorities in Scotland, the 22 unitary authorities in Wales, and the 87 unitary authorities in England as of 1 April 1998. Authorities which are too small to name on the map are numbered and listed separately.

SCOTLAND
1. ABERDEEN CITY
2. DUNDEE CITY
3. WEST DUNBARTONSHIRE
4. EAST DUNBARTONSHIRE
5. CITY OF GLASGOW
6. INVERCLYDE
7. RENFREWSHIRE
8. EAST RENFREWSHIRE
9. NORTH LANARKSHIRE
10. FALKIRK
11. CLACKMANNANSHIRE
12. WEST LOTHIAN
13. CITY OF EDINBURGH
14. MIDLOTHIAN

WALES
15. SWANSEA
16. NEATH PORT TALBOT
17. BRIDGEND
18. RHONDDA CYNON TAFF
19. MERTHYR TYDFIL
20. CAERPHILLY
21. BLAENAU GWENT
22. TORFAEN
23. CARDIFF
24. NEWPORT

ENGLAND
25. HARTLEPOOL
26. DARLINGTON
27. STOCKTON-ON-TEES
28. MIDDLESBROUGH
29. REDCAR AND CLEVELAND
30. BLACKPOOL
31. BLACKBURN WITH DARWEN
32. HALTON
33. WARRINGTON
34. KINGSTON UPON HULL
35. NORTH EAST LINCOLNSHIRE
36. STOKE-ON-TRENT
37. TELFORD AND WREKIN
38. DERBY CITY
39. CITY OF NOTTINGHAM
40. LEICESTER CITY
41. RUTLAND
42. PETERBOROUGH
43. MILTON KEYNES
44. LUTON
45. NORTH SOMERSET
46. CITY OF BRISTOL
47. BATH AND N. E. SOMERSET
48. SWINDON
49. READING
50. WOKINGHAM
51. WINDSOR AND MAIDENHEAD
52. SLOUGH
53. BRACKNELL FOREST
54. THURROCK
55. SOUTHEND-ON-SEA
56. MEDWAY
57. PLYMOUTH
58. TORBAY
59. POOLE
60. BOURNEMOUTH
61. SOUTHAMPTON
62. PORTSMOUTH
63. BRIGHTON AND HOVE

Scale

0   100 km   200 km

23

England and Wales

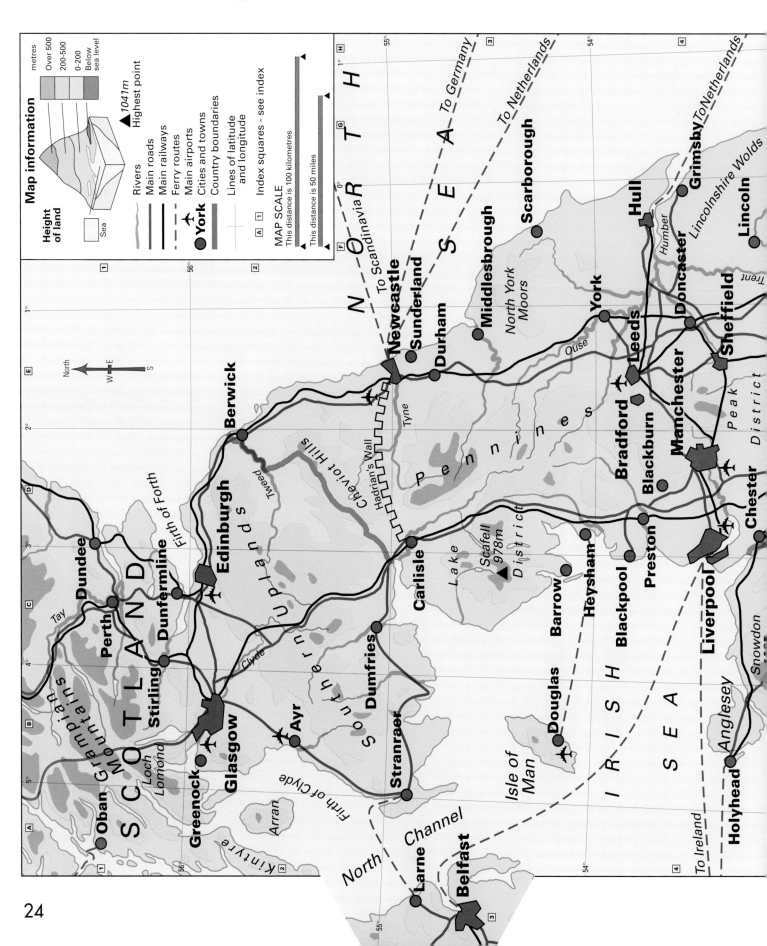

N O R T H S E A

To Scandinavia
To Germany
To Netherlands
To Netherlands

Newcastle
Sunderland
Durham
Middlesbrough
Scarborough
North York Moors
York
Ouse
Hull
Humber
Grimsby
To Netherlands
Lincolnshire Wolds
Lincoln
Leeds
Doncaster
Sheffield
Trent
Bradford
Manchester
Blackburn
Peak District

Berwick

Tweed

Cheviot Hills
Hadrian's Wall
Tyne

P e n n i n e s

Edinburgh
Firth of Forth
Dunfermline
S o u t h e r n U p l a n d s

Dundee
Tay
Perth
Stirling
Clyde
Glasgow
Greenock
Ayr

S C O T L A N D
G r a m p i a n s
Oban
Loch Lomond
Arran
Kintyre
Firth of Clyde

Dumfries
Stranraer

Carlisle
Lake District
Scafell 978m
Barrow
Heysham
Blackpool
Preston
Liverpool
Chester
Snowdon
Anglesey
Holyhead

Douglas
Isle of Man

I R I S H S E A

North Channel
Larne
Belfast
To Ireland

North

24

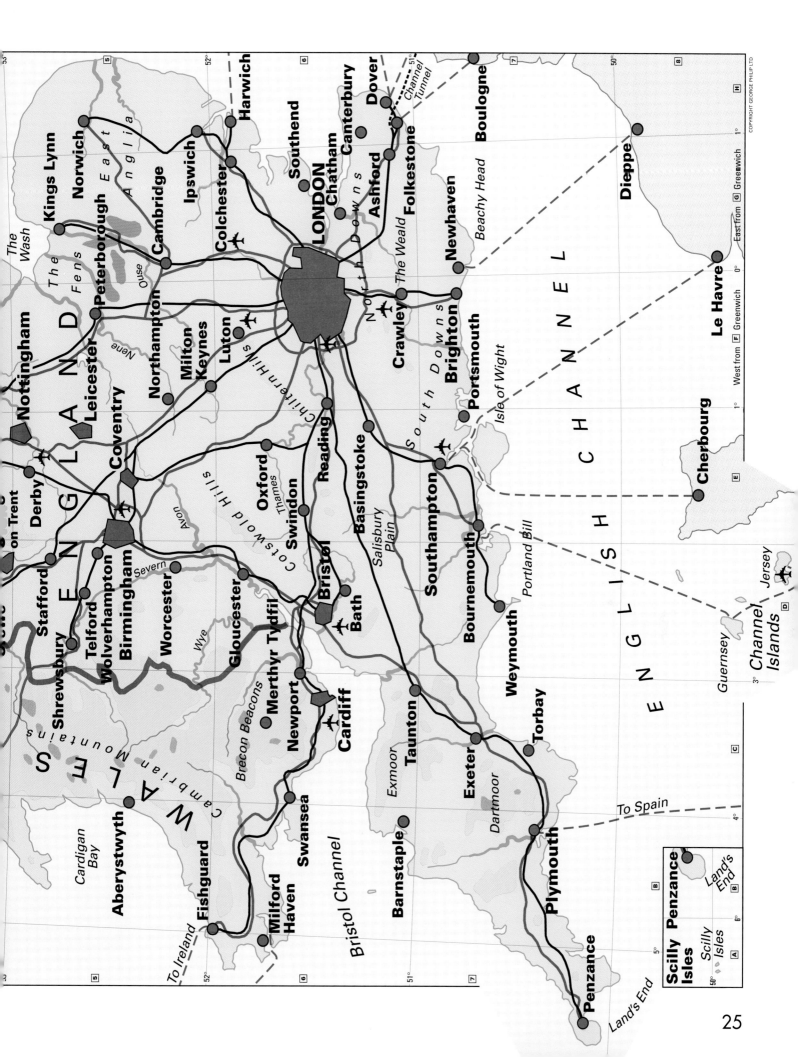

Scotland and Ireland

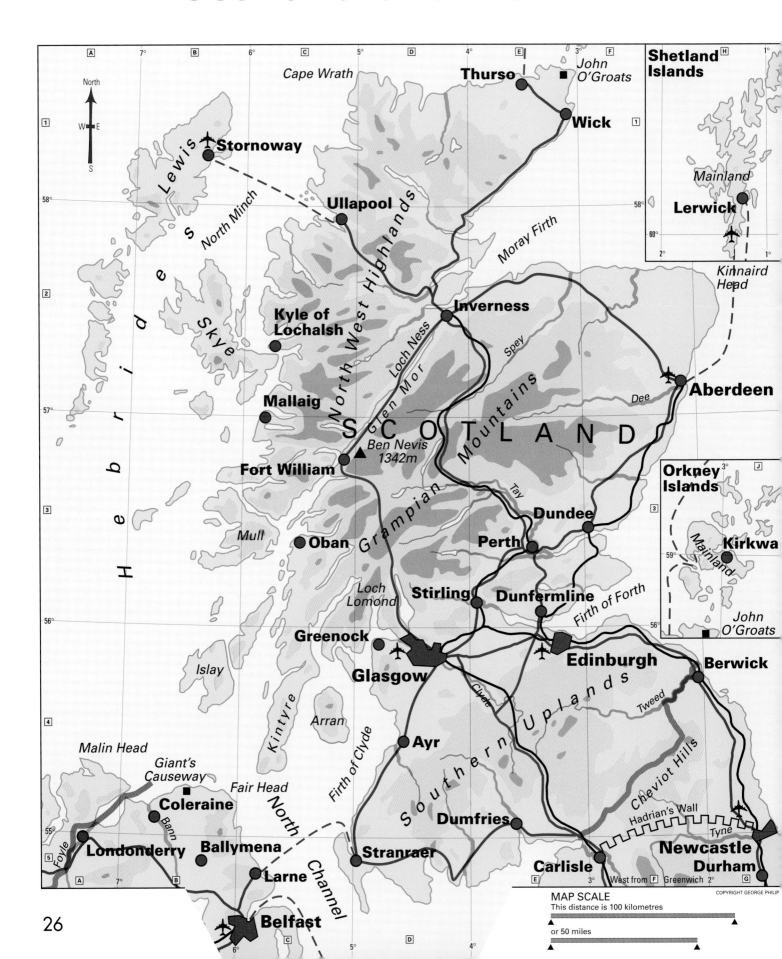

North
W—E
S

Cape Wrath

Thurso

John O'Groats

Wick

Shetland Islands

Mainland

Lerwick

Kinnaird Head

Lewis

✈ **Stornoway**

Ullapool

North Minch

Moray Firth

Skye

Kyle of Lochalsh

Inverness

Loch Ness

Spey

Mallaig

Glen Mor

S C O T L A N D

Dee

✈ **Aberdeen**

North West Highlands

▲ Ben Nevis 1342m

Fort William

Grampian Mountains

Tay

Dundee

Mull

● **Oban**

Perth

Hebrides

Orkney Islands

Mainland

Kirkwa

John O'Groats

Loch Lomond

Stirling

Dunfermline

Firth of Forth

Greenock

Glasgow

✈ **Edinburgh**

Berwick

Islay

Clyde

Southern Uplands

Tweed

Kintyre

Arran

Ayr

Cheviot Hills

Malin Head

Firth of Clyde

Giant's Causeway

Fair Head

Coleraine

Bann

Dumfries

Hadrian's Wall

North Channel

Foyle

Londonderry

Ballymena

Stranraer

Carlisle

Tyne

Newcastle
Durham

Larne

Belfast

26

MAP SCALE
This distance is 100 kilometres

or 50 miles

COPYRIGHT GEORGE PHILIP

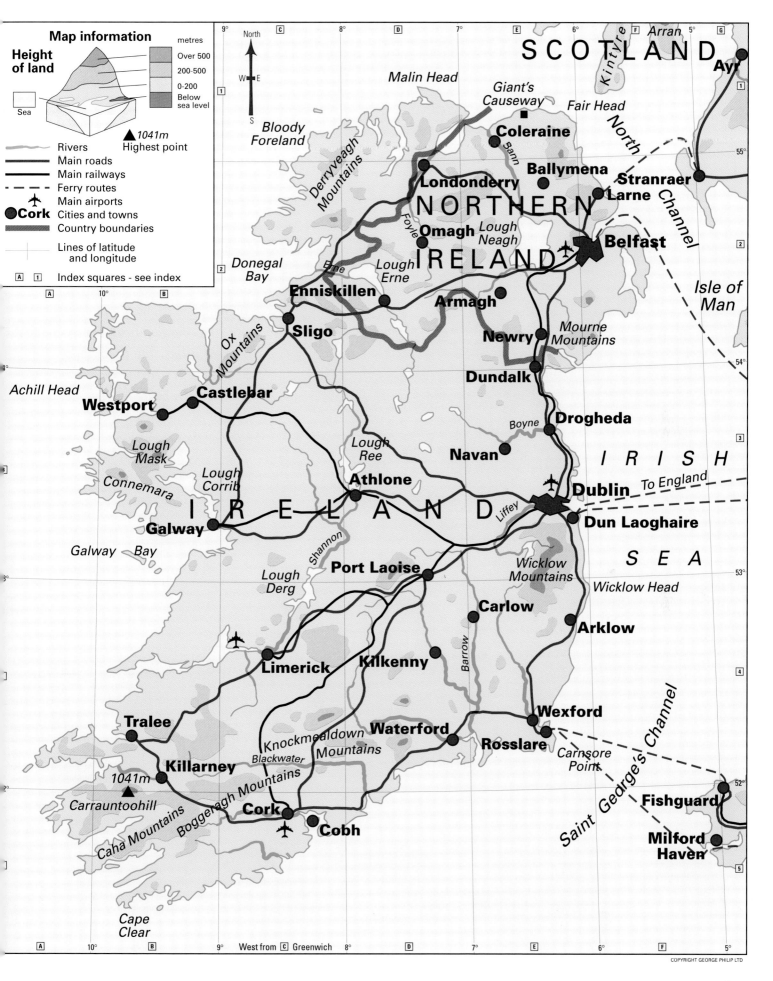

Map information

Height of land

Sea

metres	
	Over 500
	200-500
	0-200
	Below sea level

▲ 1041m Highest point

Rivers
Main roads
Main railways
Ferry routes
Main airports
●Cork Cities and towns
Country boundaries
Lines of latitude and longitude
Ⓐ ① Index squares - see index

North
W—E
S

SCOTLAND
Ayr
Kintyre
Arran

Malin Head
Giant's Causeway
Fair Head

Bloody Foreland

Coleraine
Ballymena
Stranraer
Larne

Derryveagh Mountains

Londonderry
NORTHERN

Bann

Omagh
Lough Neagh
IRELAND

Foyle

Belfast

North Channel

Donegal Bay
Erne
Lough Erne

Enniskillen

Armagh

Newry
Mourne Mountains

Isle of Man

Ox Mountains

Sligo

Dundalk

Achill Head

Westport
Castlebar

Boyne
Drogheda

IRISH

Lough Mask
Lough Corrib

Lough Ree

Navan

To England

Connemara

Athlone

Dublin

Galway

IRELAND

Liffey

Dun Laoghaire

Galway Bay

Shannon

Lough Derg

Port Laoise

Wicklow Mountains

SEA

Wicklow Head

Carlow

Arklow

Limerick

Kilkenny

Barrow

Saint George's Channel

Tralee

Knockmealdown Mountains
Waterford

Wexford

Rosslare

Killarney

Blackwater

Carnsore Point

1041m
▲
Carrauntoohill

Boggeragh Mountains

Fishguard

Caha Mountains

Cork

Cobh

Milford Haven

Cape Clear

West from Greenwich

COPYRIGHT GEORGE PHILIP LTD

27

The Earth as a planet

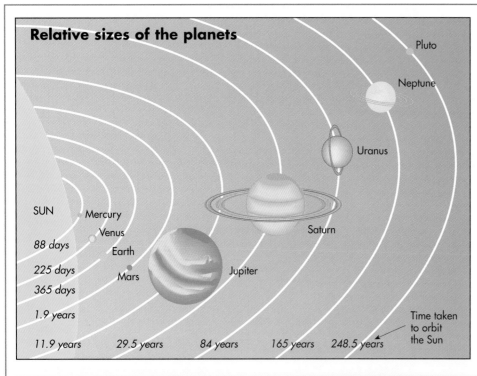

Relative sizes of the planets

Pluto
Neptune
Uranus
Saturn
SUN
Mercury
Venus
Earth
Mars
Jupiter

88 days
225 days
365 days
1.9 years
11.9 years   29.5 years   84 years   165 years   248.5 years

Time taken to orbit the Sun

The Solar System

The Earth is one of the nine planets that orbit the Sun. These two diagrams show how big the planets are, how far they are away from the Sun and how long they take to orbit the Sun. The diagram on the left shows how the planets closest to the Sun have the shortest orbits. The Earth takes 365 days (a year) to go round the Sun. The Earth is the fifth largest planet. It is much smaller than Jupiter and Saturn which are the largest planets.

Distances of the planets from the Sun in millions of kilometres

Mercury 58
Venus 108
Mars 228
Earth 150
Asteroids
Jupiter 778
Saturn 1,430
Uranus 2,870
Neptune 4,500
Pluto 5,900

Planet Earth

The Earth spins as if it is on a rod – its axis. The axis would come out of the Earth at two points. The northern point is called the North Pole and the southern point is called the South Pole. The distance between the Poles through the centre of the Earth is 12,700 km.

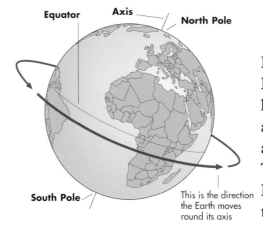

Equator   Axis   North Pole

South Pole

This is the direction the Earth moves round its axis

It takes a day (24 hours) for the Earth to rotate on its axis. It is light (day) when it faces the Sun and dark (night) when it faces away. See the diagram below. The Equator is a line round the Earth which is halfway between the Poles. It is 40,000 km long.

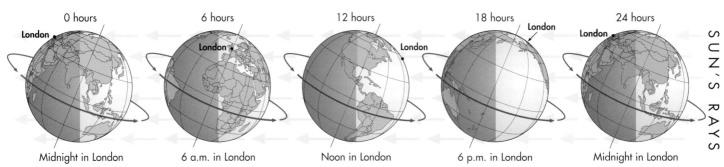

0 hours   6 hours   12 hours   18 hours   24 hours

London   London   London   London   London

Midnight in London   6 a.m. in London   Noon in London   6 p.m. in London   Midnight in London

SUN'S RAYS

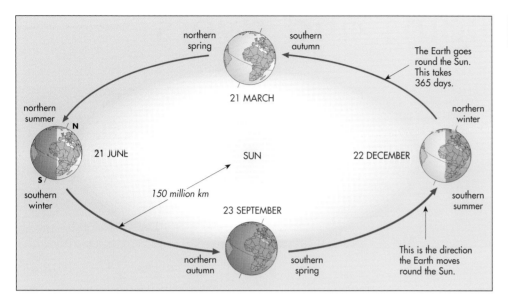

The year and seasons

The Earth is always tilted at $66\frac{1}{2}°$. It moves around the Sun. This movement gives us the seasons of the year. In June the northern hemisphere tilts towards the Sun so it is summer. Six months later, in December, the Earth has rotated halfway round the Sun. It is then summer in the southern hemisphere.

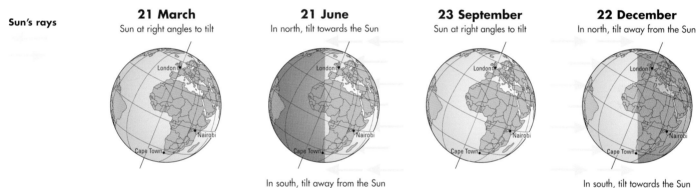

Season	Northern Spring Southern Autumn			Northern Summer Southern Winter			Northern Autumn Southern Spring			Northern Winter Southern Summer		
City	London	Nairobi	Cape Town	London	Nairobi	Cape Town	London	Nairobi	Cape Town	London	Nairobi	Cape Town
Latitude	51°N	1°S	34°S	51°N	1°S	34°S	51°N	1°S	34°S	51°N	1°S	34°S
Day length	12 hrs	12 hrs	12 hrs	16 hrs	12 hrs	10 hrs	12 hrs	12 hrs	12 hrs	8 hrs	12 hrs	14 hrs
Night length	12 hrs	12 hrs	12 hrs	8 hrs	12 hrs	14 hrs	12 hrs	12 hrs	12 hrs	16 hrs	12 hrs	10 hrs
Temperature	7°C	21°C	21°C	16°C	18°C	13°C	15°C	19°C	14°C	5°C	19°C	20°C

For example, at London in spring and autumn there are 12 hours of day and 12 hours of night. In winter this becomes 8 hours and in the summer 16 hours.

The Moon

The Moon is about a quarter the size of the Earth. It orbits the Earth in just over 27 days (almost a month). The Moon is round but we on Earth see only the parts lit by the Sun. This makes it look as if the Moon is a different shape at different times of the month. These are known as the phases of the Moon and they are shown in this diagram.

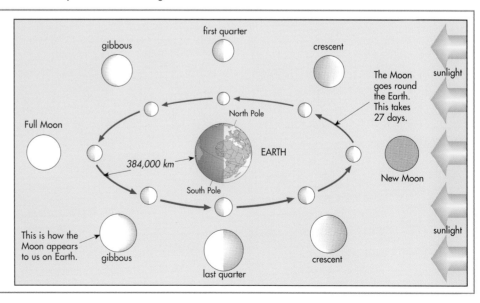

29

Mountains and rivers

The surface of the Earth is continually being shaped by movements of the Earth's crust. Volcanoes are formed and earthquakes are caused in this way. Rivers also shape the landscape as they flow on their way to the sea.

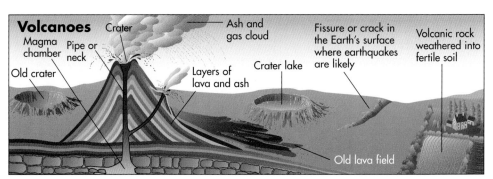

Volcanoes
Crater
Magma chamber
Pipe or neck
Old crater
Ash and gas cloud
Layers of lava and ash
Crater lake
Old lava field
Fissure or crack in the Earth's surface where earthquakes are likely
Volcanic rock weathered into fertile soil

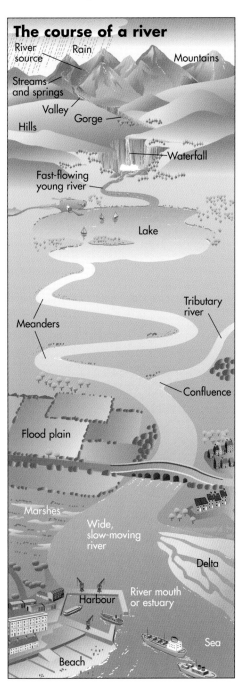

The course of a river
River source
Rain
Mountains
Streams and springs
Valley
Gorge
Hills
Waterfall
Fast-flowing young river
Lake
Tributary river
Meanders
Confluence
Flood plain
Marshes
Wide, slow-moving river
Delta
Harbour
River mouth or estuary
Sea
Beach

180 160 140 120 100 80
80
Victoria Island
Ellesmere Island
Bering Strait
Yukon
Arctic Circle
Alaska
Mount McKinley
Baffin Island
Mackenzie
Hudson Bay
Aleutian Islands
Aleutian Trench
60
Rocky Mountains
NORTH
St. Lawrence
Great Lakes
New
N O
40
Missouri
AMERICA
Mississippi
ATLA
Bermuda
Sierra Madre
Tropic of Cancer
Gulf of Mexico
O C E
20
Cuba
Milwaukee Deep
Hawaiian Islands
Caribbean Sea
West Indies
Central America
P A C I F I C
Amazon
0 Equator
Kiritimati
Equator
Galapagos Islands
Andes
Phoenix Islands
P o l y n e s i a
Marquesas islands
SOUTH
Tokelau Islands
O C E A N
AMERICA
Samoa
Society Islands
Tuamotu Archipelago
Tonga
Tahiti
Parana
20
Tonga Trench
Tubuai Islands
Tropic of Capricorn
Pitcairn Island
Easter Island
Andes
Kermadec Islands
Aconcagua
Kermadec Trench
40
Falkland Islands
Chatham Islands
Cape Horn
Antarc Penins
60
Antarctic Circle
180 160 140 120 100 80

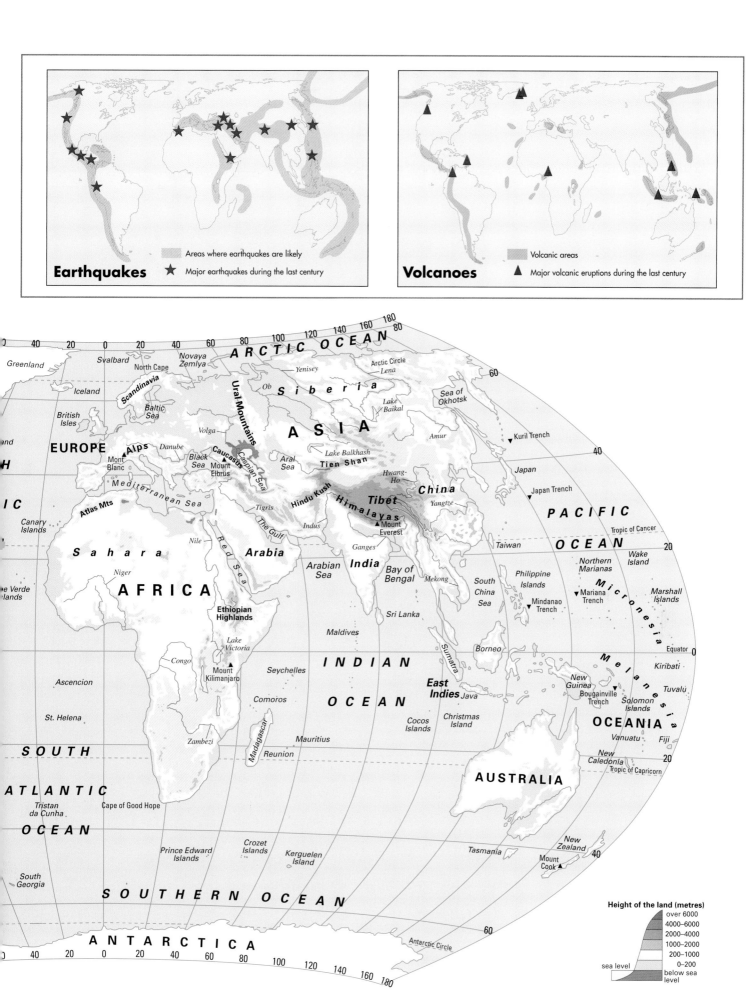

Earthquakes

Areas where earthquakes are likely

★ Major earthquakes during the last century

Volcanoes

Volcanic areas

▲ Major volcanic eruptions during the last century

Greenland · Iceland · Svalbard · North Cape · Novaya Zemlya · ARCTIC OCEAN · Arctic Circle

British Isles · Scandinavia · Baltic Sea · Ural Mountains · Ob · Yenisei · Lena · Siberia · Lake Baikal · Sea of Okhotsk

EUROPE · Alps · Mont Blanc · Danube · Volga · Black Sea · Caucasus · Mount Elbrus · Caspian Sea · Aral Sea · Tien Shan · Lake Balkhash · ASIA · Amur · Kuril Trench · Japan · 60 · 40

Atlas Mts · Mediterranean Sea · Tigris · Hindu Kush · Himalayas · Tibet · Hwang-Ho · China · Yangtze · Japan Trench · PACIFIC

Canary Islands · Sahara · Nile · Red Sea · Arabia · The Gulf · Indus · Ganges · Mount Everest · Taiwan · OCEAN · Tropic of Cancer

Verde Islands · Niger · AFRICA · Arabian Sea · India · Bay of Bengal · Mekong · South China Sea · Philippine Islands · Northern Marianas · Wake Island · Micronesia · Marshall Islands · 20

Ethiopian Highlands · Sri Lanka · Mindanao Trench · Mariana Trench

Ascension · Congo · Lake Victoria · Mount Kilimanjaro · Seychelles · Maldives · INDIAN · Sumatra · Borneo · New Guinea · Melanesia · Kiribati · Equator

St. Helena · Comoros · OCEAN · East Indies · Java · Bougainville Trench · Solomon Islands · Tuvalu

SOUTH · Zambezi · Madagascar · Mauritius · Cocos Islands · Christmas Island · OCEANIA · Vanuatu · Fiji

ATLANTIC · Reunion · New Caledonia · 20

Tristan da Cunha · Cape of Good Hope · OCEAN · AUSTRALIA · Tropic of Capricorn

Prince Edward Islands · Crozet Islands · Kerguelen Island · Tasmania · New Zealand · 40 · Mount Cook

South Georgia · SOUTHERN OCEAN · Antarctic Circle · 60

ANTARCTICA

Height of the land (metres)
- over 6000
- 4000–6000
- 2000–4000
- 1000–2000
- 200–1000
- 0–200
- sea level
- below sea level

31

Climates of the World

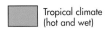 Tropical climate (hot and wet)

Heavy rainfall and high temperatures all the year with little difference between the hot and cold months.

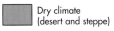 Dry climate (desert and steppe)

Many months, often years, without rain. High temperatures in the summer but cooler in winter.

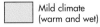 Mild climate (warm and wet)

Rain every month. Warm summers and cool winters.

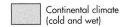 Continental climate (cold and wet)

Mild summers and very cold winters.

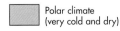 Polar climate (very cold and dry)

Very cold at all times, especially in the winter months. Very little rainfall.

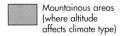 Mountainous areas (where altitude affects climate type)

Lower temperatures because the land is high. Heavy rain and snow.

Key to the climate graphs

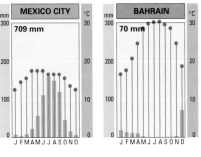

Total annual rainfall

LONDON · **593 mm**

Average monthly rainfall

Average monthly temperature in degrees C. When the temperature is below freezing the lines extend below the bottom of the graph.

Months of the year from January to December

MEXICO CITY 709 mm
BAHRAIN 70 mm
MOSCOW 575 mm · −10°C
CHURCHILL 410 mm · −28°C

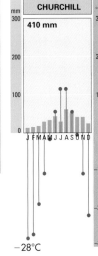
EISMITTE 5 mm · −45°C

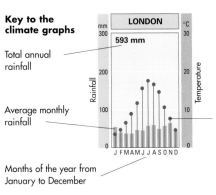
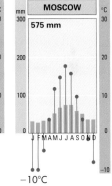
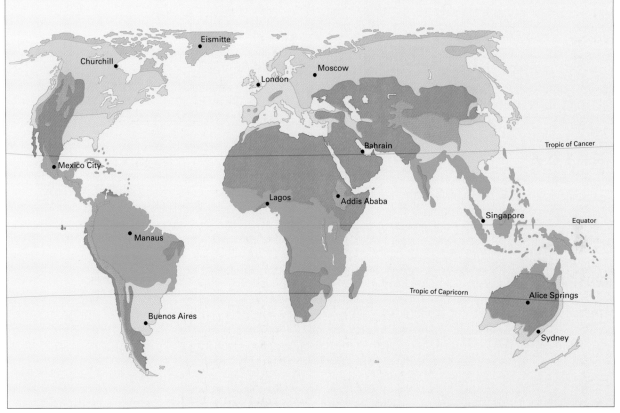

Eismitte · Churchill · London · Moscow · Mexico City · Bahrain · Lagos · Addis Ababa · Singapore · Manaus · Buenos Aires · Alice Springs · Sydney

Tropic of Cancer · Equator · Tropic of Capricorn

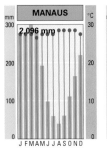 **MANAUS** 2,096 mm
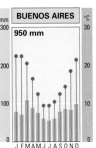 **BUENOS AIRES** 950 mm
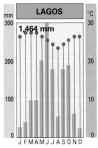 **LAGOS** 1,464 mm
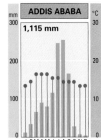 **ADDIS ABABA** 1,115 mm
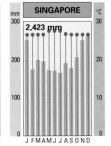 **SINGAPORE** 2,423 mm
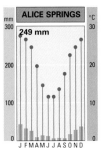 **ALICE SPRINGS** 249 mm
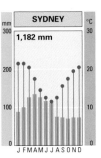 **SYDNEY** 1,182 mm

Annual rainfall

Human, plant and animal life cannot live without water. The map on the right shows how much rain falls in different parts of the world. You can see that there is a lot of rain in some places near the Equator. In other places, like the desert areas of the world, there is very little rain. Few plants or animals can survive there. There is also very little rain in the cold lands of the north.

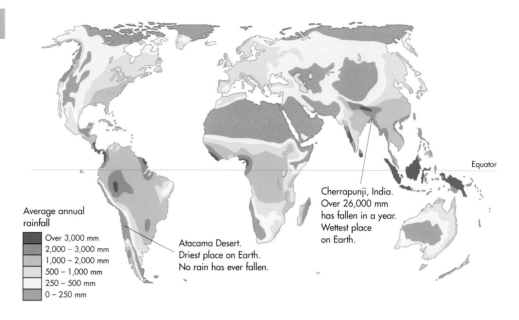

Average annual rainfall

- Over 3,000 mm
- 2,000 – 3,000 mm
- 1,000 – 2,000 mm
- 500 – 1,000 mm
- 250 – 500 mm
- 0 – 250 mm

Cherrapunji, India. Over 26,000 mm has fallen in a year. Wettest place on Earth.

Atacama Desert. Driest place on Earth. No rain has ever fallen.

Equator

Toronto

London

Northern Hemisphere – WINTER

Equator

Average temperature in January

- Over 30°C
- 20 – 30°C
- 10 – 20°C
- 0 – 10°C
- −10 – 0°C
- −20 – −10°C
- −30 – −20°C
- −40 – −30°C
- Under −40°C

Tropic of Capricorn

Cape Town

Southern Hemisphere – SUMMER

Buenos Aires

Adelaide

January temperature

In December, it is winter in the northern hemisphere. It is hot in the southern continents and cold in the northern continents. The North Pole is tilted away from the sun. It is overhead in the regions around the Tropic of Capricorn. This means that there are about 14 hours of daylight in Buenos Aires, Cape Town and Adelaide, and only about 8 hours in London and Toronto.

June temperature

In June, it is summer in the northern hemisphere and winter in the southern hemisphere. It is warmer in the northern lands and colder in the south. The North Pole is tilted towards the sun. This means that in London and Toronto there are about 16 hours of daylight, but in Buenos Aires, Cape Town and Adelaide there are just under 10 hours.

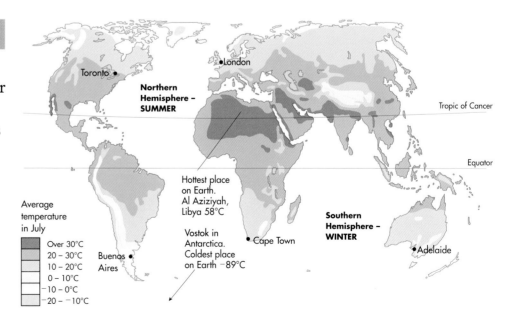

Toronto

London

Northern Hemisphere – SUMMER

Tropic of Cancer

Equator

Average temperature in July

- Over 30°C
- 20 – 30°C
- 10 – 20°C
- 0 – 10°C
- −10 – 0°C
- −20 – −10°C

Hottest place on Earth. Al Aziziyah, Libya 58°C

Vostok in Antarctica. Coldest place on Earth −89°C

Buenos Aires

Cape Town

Southern Hemisphere – WINTER

Adelaide

33

— Forests, grasslands and wastes —

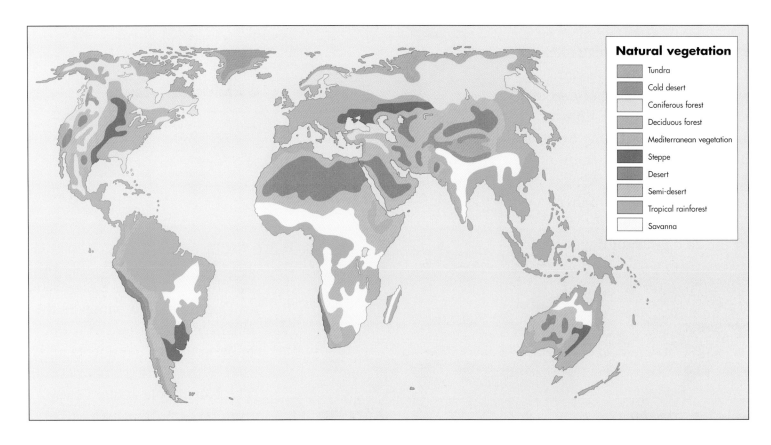

The map above shows types of vegetation around the world. The diagram below shows the types of plants which grow on mountains.

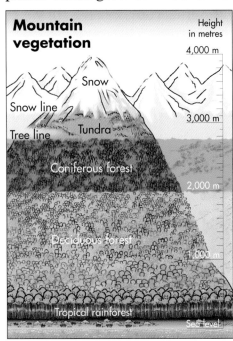

Mountain vegetation

Height in metres

4,000 m

Snow

Snow line

3,000 m

Tree line

Tundra

Coniferous forest

2,000 m

Deciduous forest

1,000 m

Tropical rainforest

Sea level

Tundra
Long, dry, cold winters. Grasses, moss, bog and dwarf trees.

Coniferous forest
Harsh winters, mild summers. Trees have leaves all year.

Mediterranean
Hot, dry summers. Mild wet winters. Plants adapt to the heat.

Desert
Rain is rare. Plants only grow at oases with underground water.

Tropical rainforest (jungle)
Very hot and wet all the year. Tall trees and lush vegetation.

Cold desert
Very cold with little rain or snow. No plants can grow.

Deciduous forest
Rain all year, cool winters. Trees shed leaves in winter.

Steppe
Some rain with a dry season. Grasslands with some trees.

Semi-desert
Poor rains, sparse vegetation. Grass with a few small trees.

Savanna
Mainly dry, but lush grass grows when the rains come.

Natural vegetation

- Tundra
- Cold desert
- Coniferous forest
- Deciduous forest
- Mediterranean vegetation
- Steppe
- Desert
- Semi-desert
- Tropical rainforest
- Savanna

Tundra

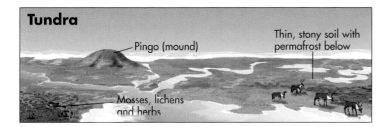

Pingo (mound)

Thin, stony soil with permafrost below

Mosses, lichens and herbs

Cold desert

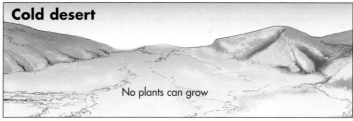

No plants can grow

Coniferous forest

Evergreen conifers (spruces and firs)

Young tree saplings and small shrubs

Carpet of pine needles

Ferns and brambles on edge of forest

Yearly cycle of a deciduous forest

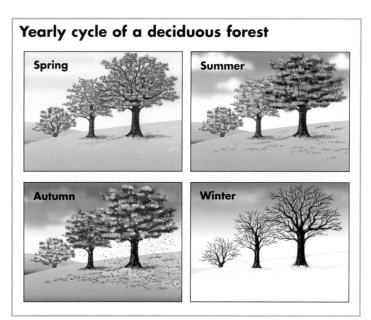

Spring

Summer

Autumn

Winter

Mediterranean

Small stunted trees

Scrub

Steppe

There are many plants in the steppe grasslands.

People planting crops damages the natural habitat.

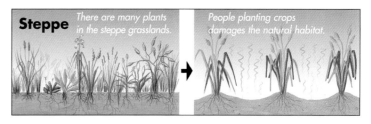

Tropical rainforest

Scattered trees with umbrella-shaped tops grow the highest.

Main layer of tall trees growing close together.

Creepers grow up the trees to reach the sunlight.

Ferns, mosses and small plants grow closest to the ground.

Desert

Sand blown into dunes by the wind

Palm trees

Cactus

Oasis

Semi-desert

Joshua trees

Grass and bush

Savanna

Dry season

Wet season

- Agriculture, forests and fishing -

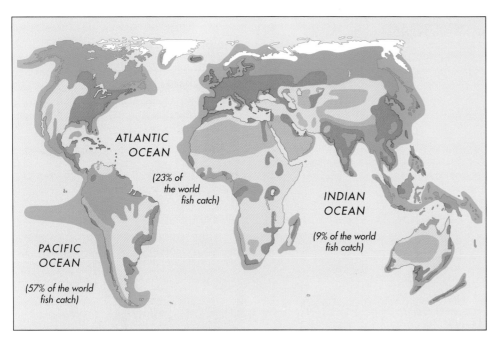

ATLANTIC
OCEAN

*(23% of
the world
fish catch)*

INDIAN
OCEAN

*(9% of the world
fish catch)*

PACIFIC
OCEAN

*(57% of the world
fish catch)*

How the land is used

Forest areas with timber.
Some hunting and fishing.
Agriculture in the tropics.

Deserts and wastelands. Some
small areas of agriculture in oases
or places that have been irrigated.

Animal farming on large farms
(ranches)

Farming of crops and animals on
large and small farms

Main fishing areas

The importance of agriculture

Over half the people work in agriculture

Between a quarter and half the people
work in agriculture

Between one in ten and a quarter of
the people work in agriculture

Less than one in ten of the people work
in agriculture

● Countries which depend on agriculture
for over half their income

A hundred years ago about 80%
of the world's population worked
in agriculture. Today it is only
about 40% but agriculture is still
very important in some countries.

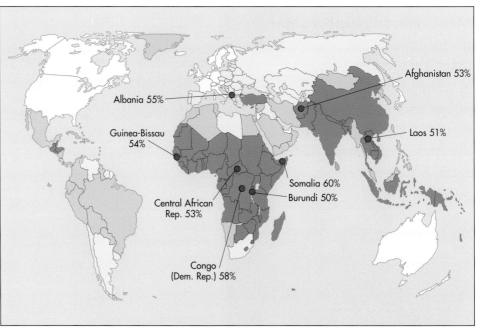

Afghanistan 53%

Albania 55%

Guinea-Bissau
54%

Laos 51%

Somalia 60%

Burundi 50%

Central African
Rep. 53%

Congo
(Dem. Rep.) 58%

Methods of fishing

There are two types
of sea fishing:

1. **Deep-sea fishing**
using large trawlers
which often stay at
sea for many weeks.

2. **Inshore fishing**
using small boats,
traps and nets up to
70 km from the coast.

Inshore fishing

Deep-sea fishing (drifter)

Fishing vessels

(trawler)

Seine net to catch
herring, tuna and
mackerel

Trawl net to
catch fish
near the sea
bed (sole,
cod and
haddock)

Lobster
pots

Fish trap

Sonar is used
to find fish

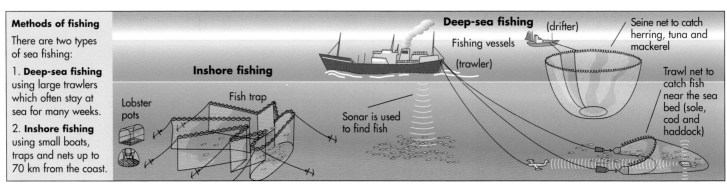

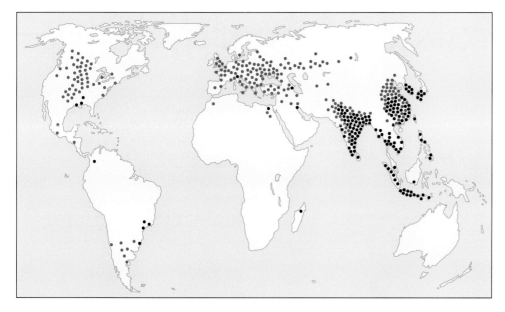

Wheat and rice

- One dot stands for 2 million tonnes of wheat produced
- One dot stands for 2 million tonnes of rice produced

Wheat is the main cereal crop grown in cooler regions. Rice is the main food for over half the people in the world. It is grown in water in paddy fields in tropical areas. Over a third of the world's rice is grown in China.

Cattle and sheep

- One dot stands for 10 million cattle
- One dot stands for 10 million sheep

Meat, milk and leather come from cattle. The map shows that they are kept in most parts of the world except where it is hot or very cold. Sheep are kept in cooler regions and they can live on poorer grassland than cows. Sheep are reared for meat and wool.

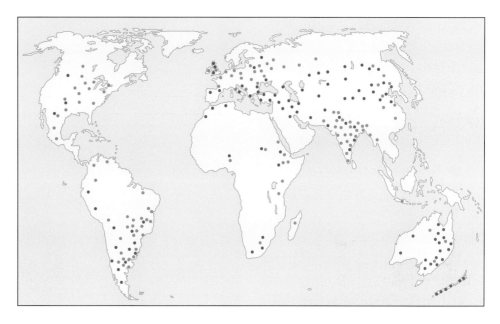

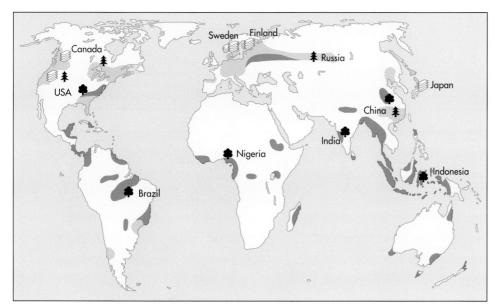

Timber

- Main areas where trees are grown for hardwoods (non-coniferous)
- Main areas where trees are grown for softwoods (coniferous)

Countries producing over 5% of
- 🍀 the world's hardwood
- 🌲 the world's softwood
- the world's wood pulp

Trees are cut down to make timber. Softwood trees such as pines and firs often have cones so they are called coniferous. Some trees are chopped up into wood pulp which is used to make paper.

37

Minerals and energy

Important metals

■ Iron ore

▲ Bauxite

● Copper

Iron is the most important metal in manufacturing. It is mixed with other metals to make steel which is used for ships, cars and machinery. Bauxite ore is used to make aluminium. Aluminium is light and strong. It is used to make aeroplanes. Copper is used for electric wires, and also to make brass and bronze.

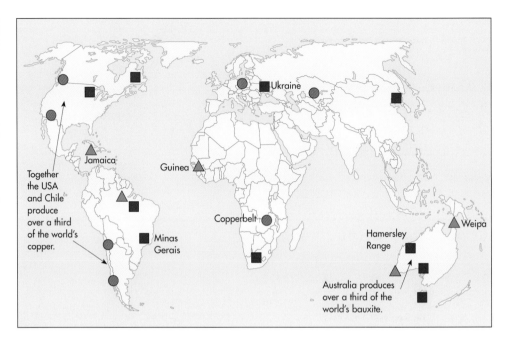

Together the USA and Chile produce over a third of the world's copper.

Ukraine

Jamaica

Guinea

Copperbelt

Minas Gerais

Weipa

Hamersley Range

Australia produces over a third of the world's bauxite.

Precious metals and minerals

⬮ Gold

★ Silver

◆ Diamonds

Some minerals like gold, silver and diamonds are used to make jewellery. They are also important in industry. Diamonds are the hardest mineral and so they are used on tools that cut or grind. Silver is used in photography to coat film, and to make electrical goods. Gold is used in the electronics industry.

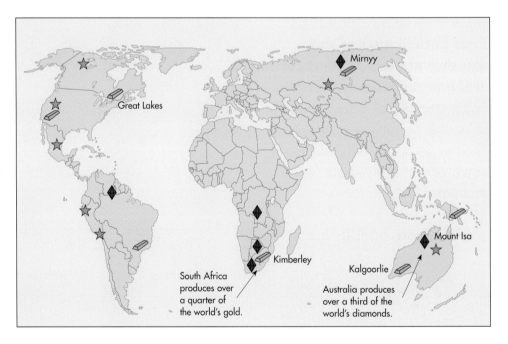

Mirnyy

Great Lakes

South Africa produces over a quarter of the world's gold.

Kimberley

Kalgoorlie

Mount Isa

Australia produces over a third of the world's diamonds.

There are over 70 different types of metals and minerals in the world. The maps above show the main countries where some of the most important ones are mined. After mining, metals and fuels are often exported to other countries where they are manufactured into goods. The map on the left shows which countries depend most on mining for their exports and wealth. These countries are coloured red.

Oil and gas

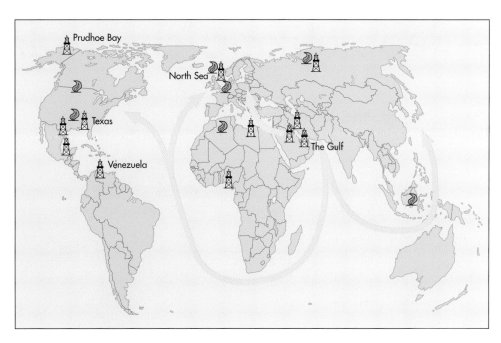

⛏	Oilfields
🌀	Natural gasfields
➡	Main routes for transporting oil and gas by tanker

Crude oil is drilled from deep in the Earth's crust. The oil is then refined so that it can be used in different industries. Oil is used to make petrol and is also very important in the chemical industry. Natural gas is often found in the same places as oil.

Coal

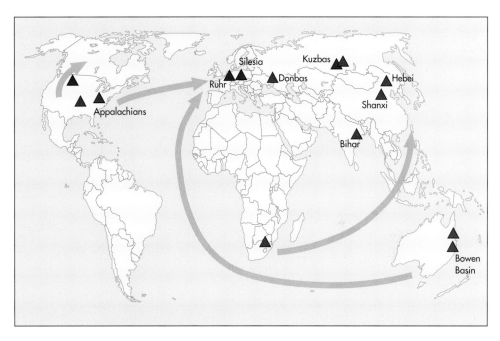

▲	Lignite (soft brown coal)
▲	Hard coal (bituminous)
➡	Main routes for transporting coal

Coal is a fuel that comes from forests and swamps that rotted millions of years ago and have been crushed by layers of rock. The coal is cut out of the rock from deep mines and also from open-cast mines where the coal is nearer the surface. The oldest type of coal is hard. The coal formed more recently is softer.

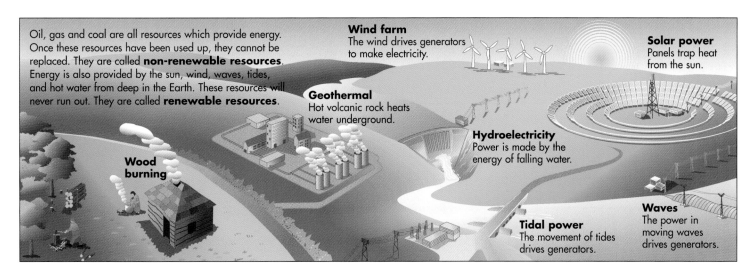

Oil, gas and coal are all resources which provide energy. Once these resources have been used up, they cannot be replaced. They are called **non-renewable resources**. Energy is also provided by the sun, wind, waves, tides, and hot water from deep in the Earth. These resources will never run out. They are called **renewable resources**.

Wind farm
The wind drives generators to make electricity.

Solar power
Panels trap heat from the sun.

Geothermal
Hot volcanic rock heats water underground.

Hydroelectricity
Power is made by the energy of falling water.

Wood burning

Tidal power
The movement of tides drives generators.

Waves
The power in moving waves drives generators.

– Peoples and cities of the World –

Where people live

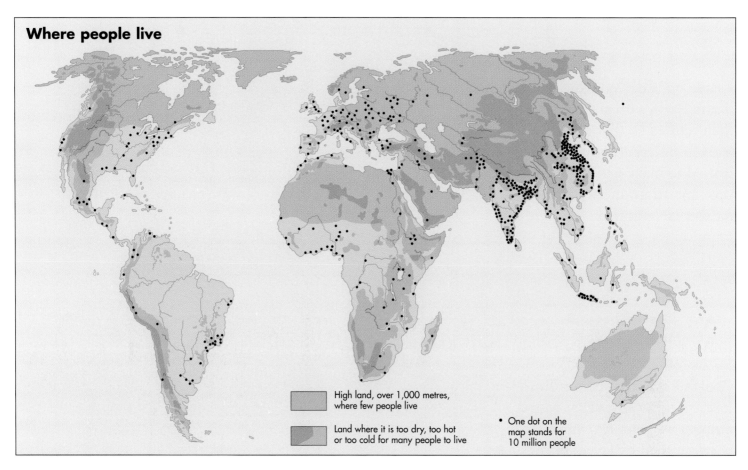

High land, over 1,000 metres, where few people live

Land where it is too dry, too hot or too cold for many people to live

• One dot on the map stands for 10 million people

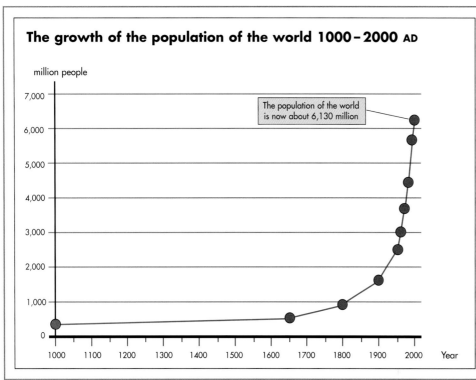

The growth of the population of the world 1000–2000 AD

million people

The population of the world is now about 6,130 million

7,000

6,000

5,000

4,000

3,000

2,000

1,000

0

1000 1100 1200 1300 1400 1500 1600 1700 1800 1900 2000 Year

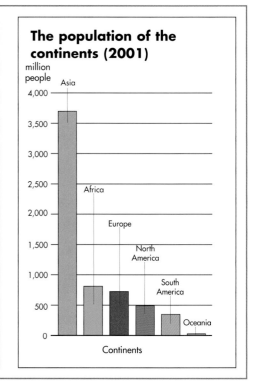

The population of the continents (2001)

million people

Asia

4,000

3,500

3,000

2,500 Africa

2,000 Europe

1,500 North America

1,000 South America

500 Oceania

0

Continents

The world's largest cities

(population in millions)

New York	21
Tokyo	18
Mexico City	16
Mumbai (Bombay)	16
Los Angeles	16
Shanghai	15
Kolkata (Calcutta)	13
Beijing	12
Jakarta	12
Delhi	12
Buenos Aires	11
Tianjin	11
Paris	11
Sao Paulo	10
Seoul	10
Lagos	10
Karachi	9
Manila	9
Chicago	9
Istanbul	9
Moscow	8
Dhaka	8
London	8
Washington	8
Bangkok	8

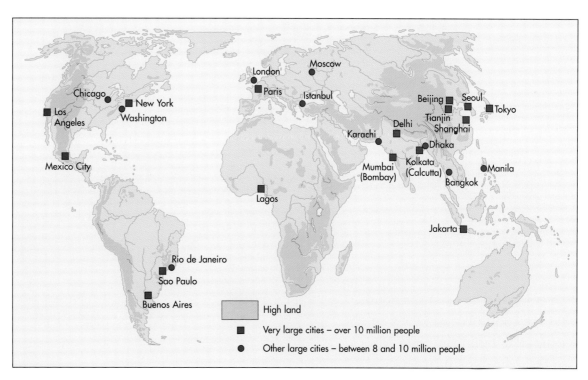

High land

■ Very large cities – over 10 million people

● Other large cities – between 8 and 10 million people

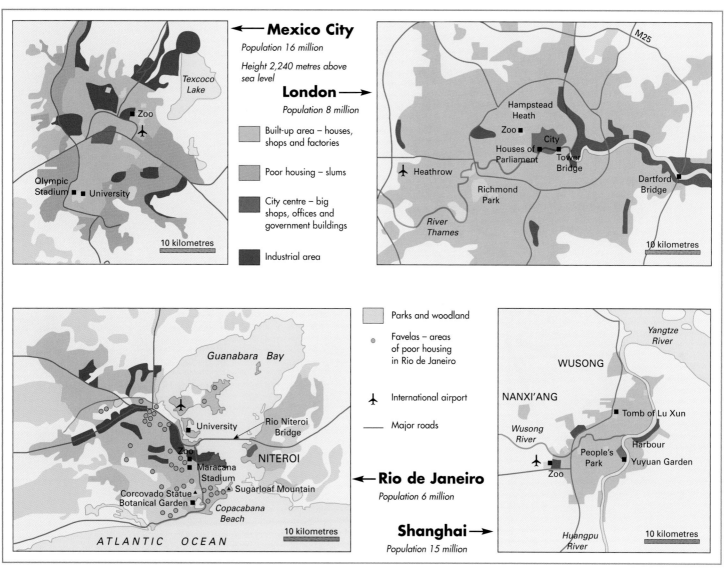

Mexico City

Population 16 million

Height 2,240 metres above sea level

London

Population 8 million

Built-up area – houses, shops and factories

Poor housing – slums

City centre – big shops, offices and government buildings

Industrial area

Parks and woodland

Favelas – areas of poor housing in Rio de Janeiro

International airport

Major roads

Rio de Janeiro

Population 6 million

Shanghai

Population 15 million

41

World transport

Seaways

— Main shipping routes

■ The biggest seaports in the world (over a hundred million tonnes of cargo handled a year)

● Other big seaports

▨ Ice and icebergs in the sea all the time, or for some part of the year

— Large ships can sail on these rivers

Sea transport is used for goods that are too bulky or heavy to go by air. The main shipping routes are between North America, Europe and the Far East.

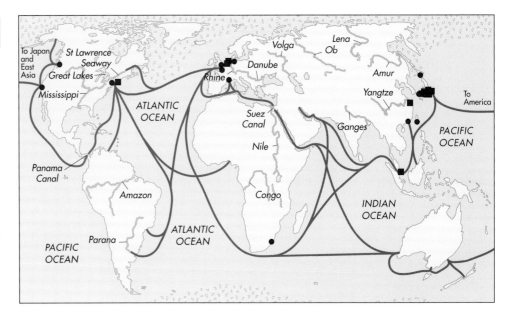

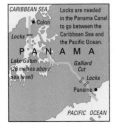

The Panama Canal

Opened in 1914
82 km long
13,000 ships a year

The Suez Canal

Opened in 1870
162 km long
17,000 ships a year

These two important canals cut through narrow pieces of land. Can you work out how much shorter the journeys are by using the canals?

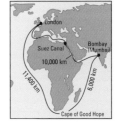

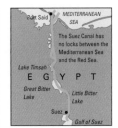

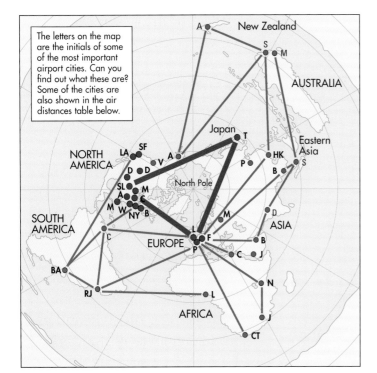

The letters on the map are the initials of some of the most important airport cities. Can you find out what these are? Some of the cities are also shown in the air distances table below.

● Large international airports (over 20 million passengers a year)

● Other important airports

▬ Heavily used air routes

— Other important air routes

Airways

This map has the North Pole at its centre. It shows how much air traffic connects Europe, North America, Japan and Eastern Asia. You can see the long distances in the USA and Russia that are covered by air.

Air distances (kilometres)

	Buenos Aires	Cape Town	London	Los Angeles	New York	Sydney	Tokyo
Buenos Aires		6,880	11,128	9,854	8,526	11,760	18,338
Cape Town	6,880		9,672	16,067	12,551	10,982	14,710
London	11,128	9,672		8,752	5,535	17,005	9,584
Los Angeles	9,854	16,067	8,752		3,968	12,052	8,806
New York	8,526	12,551	5,535	3,968		16,001	10,869
Sydney	11,760	10,982	17,005	12,052	16,001		7,809
Tokyo	18,338	14,710	9,584	8,806	10,869	7,809	

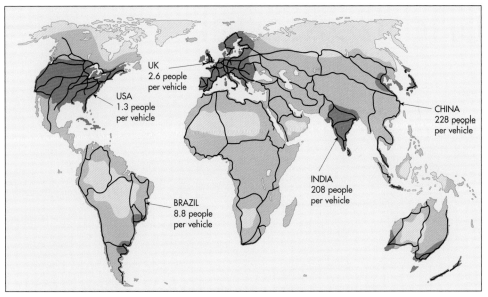

Roads

■	Many roads and motorways
▨	Not many roads, few with hard surfaces and many only tracks. Many roads are through-routes.
□	No roads or very few roads
—	Important long-distance roads

This map shows some of the major roads that link important cities and ports. It also shows how many people there are in proportion to the number of vehicles in some countries.

UK
2.6 people
per vehicle

USA
1.3 people
per vehicle

CHINA
228 people
per vehicle

BRAZIL
8.8 people
per vehicle

INDIA
208 people
per vehicle

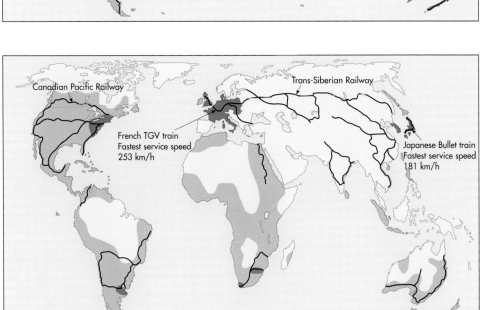

Canadian Pacific Railway

Trans-Siberian Railway

French TGV train
Fastest service speed
253 km/h

Japanese Bullet train
Fastest service speed
181 km/h

Railways

■	Many passenger and goods lines
▨	Scattered railways often taking goods to and from parts of the coast
□	No rail services or very few rail services
—	Important long-distance railways

This map shows some of the important long-distance railways in the world. Railways are often used for transporting goods between cities and to ports.

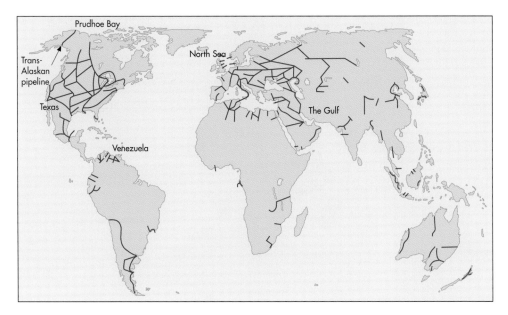

Prudhoe Bay

North Sea

Trans-Alaskan pipeline

Texas

The Gulf

Venezuela

Pipelines

—	Oil and gas pipelines

Pipelines are used for moving oil or gas. Oil and gas are moved to where they will be used or to seaports for loading into tankers to be taken across the sea. The Trans-Alaskan pipeline was built because tankers cannot cross ice. The main oil and gas producing areas of the world are shown on page 39.

43

Planet in danger

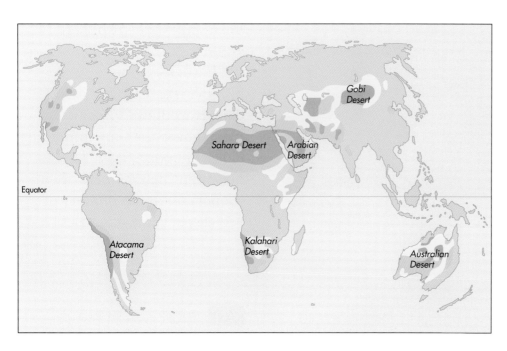

Expanding deserts

Existing deserts

Expanding deserts

Areas with the risk of becoming desert

In some parts of the world deserts are expanding. This is because trees are cut down and there are too many animals grazing the land near the desert edge. Soils are not dug properly and they become poorer. Gradually farming becomes impossible and the land becomes desert.

Forests in danger

Tropical forests today

Tropical forests that have been destroyed or opened up in large areas this century

Softwood forests that have suffered damage from air pollution, or cutting down too many trees

The tropical forests are so big that they affect the climate of the whole world. Their area is getting smaller. They are being cut down for wood and to clear land for ranching, 'slash and burn' farming and mining.

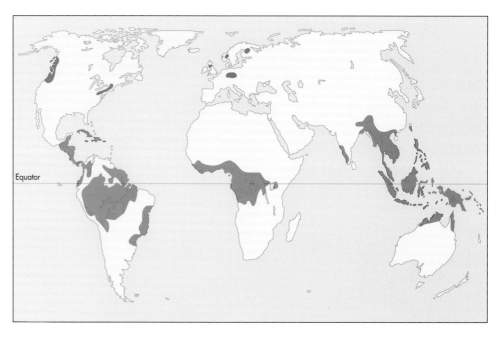

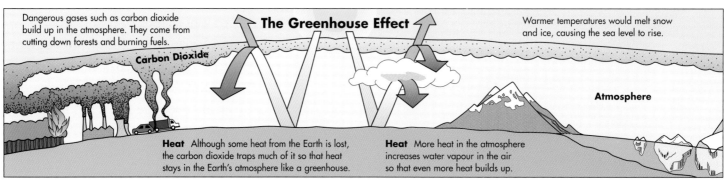

Dangerous gases such as carbon dioxide build up in the atmosphere. They come from cutting down forests and burning fuels.

The Greenhouse Effect

Warmer temperatures would melt snow and ice, causing the sea level to rise.

Carbon Dioxide

Atmosphere

Heat Although some heat from the Earth is lost, the carbon dioxide traps much of it so that heat stays in the Earth's atmosphere like a greenhouse.

Heat More heat in the atmosphere increases water vapour in the air so that even more heat builds up.

Sources of river pollution

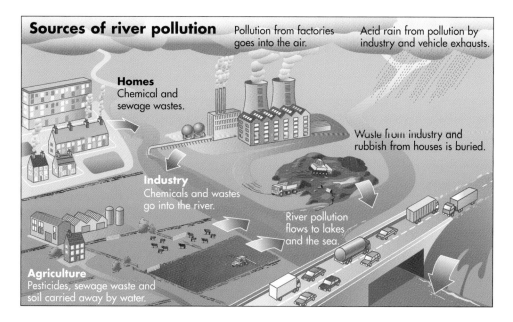

Pollution from factories goes into the air.

Acid rain from pollution by industry and vehicle exhausts.

Homes
Chemical and sewage wastes.

Waste from industry and rubbish from houses is buried.

Industry
Chemicals and wastes go into the river.

River pollution flows to lakes and the sea.

Agriculture
Pesticides, sewage waste and soil carried away by water.

Pollution

This diagram shows some of the ways that we pollute the land, rivers, sea and air around us. Air pollution causes the Earth's atmosphere to become warmer. This is called the 'Greenhouse Effect' (see the diagram at the bottom of the opposite page). The world's climate is gradually changing because of the 'Greenhouse Effect'.

Sea and river pollution

- Bad pollution of the sea and lakes
- Other sea and lake pollution
- Frequent pollution of the sea from oil on shipping routes
- Major oil tanker spills
- Badly polluted rivers

Rubbish and sewage are dumped into the rivers and the sea (see the diagram above). Plants and animals in the water die. Oil tankers sometimes sink and their oil escapes.

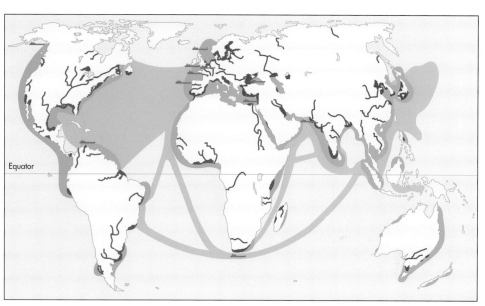

Equator

Air pollution

- Areas where rain can be very acidic
- Large cities that often have unhealthy air

Coal, oil and gas burned in power stations have sulphur and nitrogen in their smoke. This goes into the sky and it combines with rain to make acids (see the diagram on page 21). The acid kills trees and plants, and fish in the rivers and lakes.

Equator

45

Rich and poor

All countries have both rich and poor people but some countries have more poor people than others. The amount of food that people have to eat and the age that they die can often depend on where they live in the world. The world can be divided into two parts – the North and the South.

The richer countries are in the North and the poorer countries are in the South. The map below shows the dividing line, with Australia and New Zealand in the North. The list on the right shows some contrasts between the North and the South. Some of these contrasts can be seen in the maps on these pages.

North	South
Rich	Poor
Healthy	Poor health
Educated	Poor education
Well fed	Poorly fed
Small families	Large families
Many industries	Few industries
Few farmers	Many farmers
Give aid	Receive aid

The South has over three-quarters of the world's population but less than a quarter of its wealth.

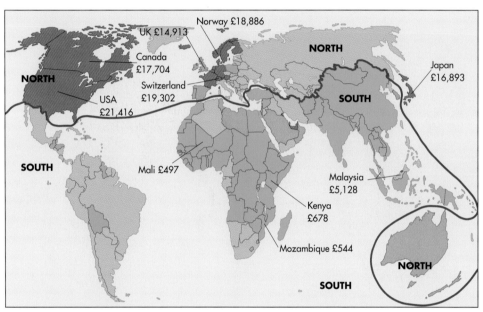

Income

	Very rich countries
	Rich countries
	Poor countries
	Very poor countries

The map shows how much money there is to spend on each person in a country. This is called income per person – this is worked out by dividing the wealth of a country by its population. The map gives examples of rich and poor countries.

How long do people live?

This is the average age when people die

	Over 75 years
	60 – 75 years
	Under 60 years

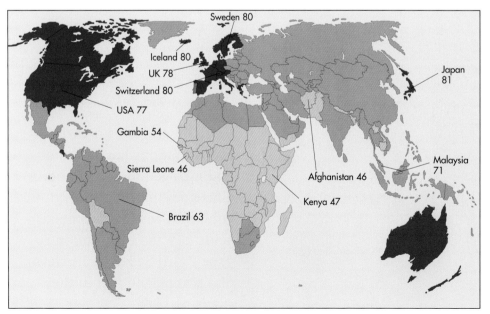

The average age of death is called life expectancy. In the world as a whole, the average life expectancy is 65 years. Some of the highest and lowest ages of death are shown on the map.

Food and famine

Below the amount

Above the amount

Over a third above the amount

★ Major famines since 1980

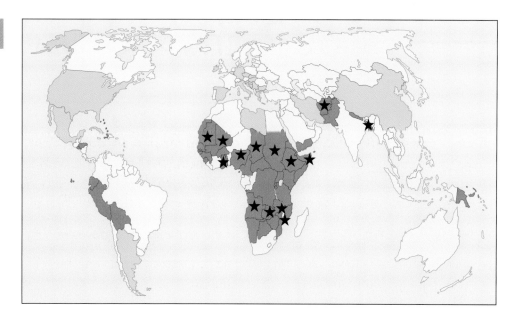

If people do not have enough to eat they become unhealthy. This map shows where in the world people have less than and more than the amount of food they need to live a healthy life.

Reading and writing

Over half the adults

Between a quarter and a half of the adults

Less than a quarter of the adults

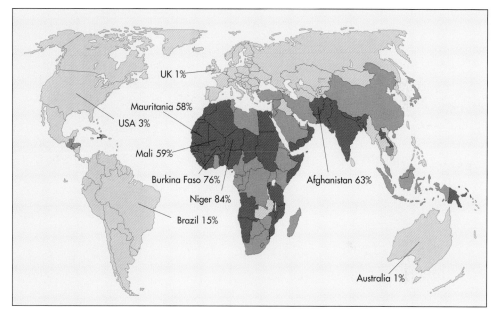

UK 1%

Mauritania 58%

USA 3%

Mali 59%

Burkina Faso 76%

Afghanistan 63%

Niger 84%

Brazil 15%

Australia 1%

The map shows the proportion of adults in each country who cannot read or write a simple sentence. Can you think of some reasons why more people cannot read or write in some places in the world than in others?

Development aid

Over £25 received per person each year

Up to £25 received per person each year

Up to £25 given per person each year

Over £25 given per person each year

Countries that receive or give no aid

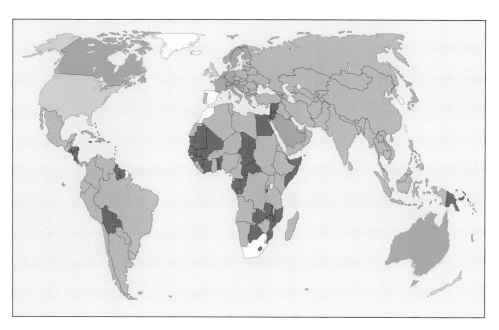

Some countries receive aid from other countries. Money is one type of aid. It is used to help with food, health and education problems. The map shows how much different countries give or receive.

Countries of the World

North America

(see pages 58–59)

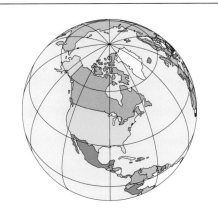

South America

(see pages 60–61)

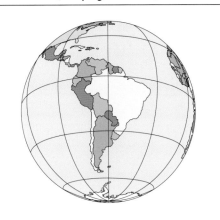

Africa

(see pages 54–55)

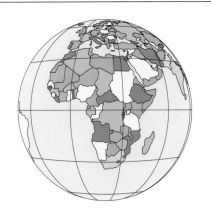

These pages show different maps of the world. The large map shows the world cut through the Pacific Ocean and opened out on to flat paper. The smaller maps of the continents are views of the globe looking down on each of the continents, as they would appear from a spacecraft 32,000 kilometres above the Earth's surface. Larger maps of the continents appear on the following pages. They show more cities than on this map

■ Cities with more than 10 million people

Europe

(see pages 50–51)

Asia

(see pages 52–53)

Oceania

(see pages 56–57)

GREENLAND (Den.)

Svalbard (Norway)

Arctic Circle

ICELAND

R U S S I A

60

NORWAY SWEDEN FINLAND

UNITED KINGDOM

DENMARK

ESTONIA LATVIA LITHUANIA

Moscow

IRELAND

London

NETH. GERMANY POLAND BELG. LUX. CZECH. FRANCE AUSTRIA SWITZ. SLOV. CR. B.-H. ITALY

UKRAINE MOLD.

BELARUS

KAZAKHSTAN

MONGOLIA

40

NORTH KOREA

JAPAN

Beijing (Peking)

Tokyo

Seoul SOUTH KOREA

Osaka

ROMANIA YUG. BULGARIA ALB. MAC.

GEORGIA ARM. AZER.

UZBEKISTAN

KYRGYZSTAN

C H I N A

Shanghai

PORTUGAL SPAIN

GREECE

TURKEY

TURKMENISTAN

TAJIKISTAN

P A C I F I C

Azores (Port.)

CYPRUS LEB. SYRIA ISRAEL JORDAN

Tehran I R A N

AFGHANISTAN

Delhi

NEPAL BHUTAN

Tropic of Cancer

Canary Is. (Spain)

MOROCCO

TUNISIA

IRAQ KUWAIT

PAKISTAN

Karachi

BANGLA- DESH

20

WESTERN SAHARA

ALGERIA

LIBYA

Cairo EGYPT

BAHRAIN QATAR SAUDI U.A.E. ARABIA OMAN

Kolkata (Calcutta)

Dacca

O C E A N

MAURITANIA

MALI NIGER

CHAD

SUDAN

ERITREA YEMEN

Mumbai (Bombay)

I N D I A

BURMA (Myanmar)

TAIWAN

LAOS

Chennai (Madras)

THAI- LAND

Manila PHILIPPINES

NORTHERN MARIANAS

Guam (U.S.A.)

MARSHALL IS.

CAPE VERDE IS.

SENEGAL GAMBIA GUINEA-BISSAU GUINEA SIERRA LEONE LIBERIA

BURKINA-FASO IVORY COAST

GHANA

BENIN TOGO NIGERIA Lagos

DJIBOUTI

CENTRAL AFRICAN REP.

ETHIOPIA

SOMALI REP.

MALDIVES

SRI LANKA

Bangkok CAMBODIA VIETNAM

BRUNEI

FEDERATED STATES OF MICRONESIA

PALAU

CAMEROON

EQUATORIAL GUINEA

GABON CONGO

CONGO (Dem. Rep. of the)

UGANDA RWANDA BURUNDI

KENYA

SEYCHELLES

I N D I A N

MALAYSIA SINGAPORE

Borneo

Sumatra

I N D O N E S I A

New Guinea

PAPUA NEW GUINEA

SOLOMON IS.

Equator

KIRIBATI

Ascencion (U.K.)

CABINDA

TANZANIA

Jakarta

O C E A N

EAST TIMOR

TUVALU

St. Helena (U.K.)

ANGOLA

ZAMBIA

MALAWI

Cocos Islands (Australia)

Christmas Island (Australia)

VANUATU

FIJI

S O U T H

NAMIBIA

ZIMBABWE BOTSWANA

MOZAMBIQUE

MADAGASCAR

COMOROS

MAURITIUS

Réunion (Fr.)

New Caledonia (Fr.)

20

Tropic of Capricorn

A T L A N T I C

SWAZILAND

SOUTH AFRICA

LESOTHO

A U S T R A L I A

Tristan da Cunha (U.K.)

O C E A N

Prince Edward Islands (South Africa)

Crozet Is. (Fr.)

Kerguelen Is. (Fr.)

NEW ZEALAND

40

South Georgia (U.K.)

S O U T H E R N   O C E A N

A n t a r c t i c a

Antarctic Circle

60

West from Greenwich East from Greenwich

ALB.	= Albania	LEB.	= Lebanon
ARM.	= Armenia	LUX.	= Luxembourg
AZER.	= Azerbaijan	MAC.	= Macedonia
BELG.	= Belgium	MOLD.	= Moldova
B.-H.	= Bosnia-Herzegovina	NETH.	= Netherlands
CR.	= Croatia	SLOV.	= Slovenia
CZECH.	= Czech Republic	SWITZ.	= Switzerland
DOM. REP.	= Dominican Republic	U.A.E.	= United Arab Emirates
HUNG.	= Hungary	YUG.	= Yugoslavia

Europe

Largest countries – by area

(thousand square kilometres)

Russia	17,075
Ukraine	604
France	552
Spain	505

Largest countries – by population

(million people)

Russia	145
Germany	83
United Kingdom	60
France	60

Largest cities

(million people)

Paris (FRANCE)	11.1
Moscow (RUSSIA)	8.4
London (UK)	8.1
St Petersburg (RUSSIA)	4.2

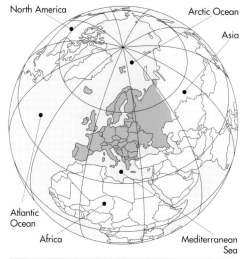

- *Europe is the second smallest continent. It is one fifth the size of Asia. Australia is slightly smaller than Europe.*
- *Great Britain is the largest island in Europe. Iceland is the second largest and Ireland is the third largest.*

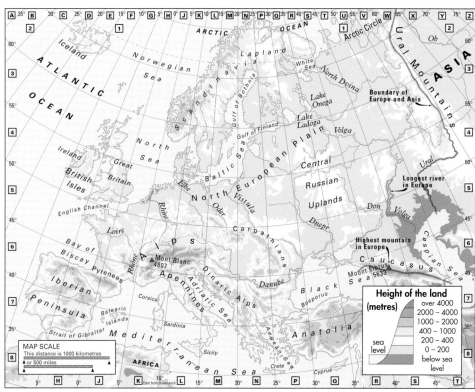

MAP SCALE
This distance is 1000 kilometres
or 500 miles

Height of the land
(metres)
- over 4000
- 2000 – 4000
- 1000 – 2000
- 400 – 1000
- 200 – 400
- sea level   0 – 200
- below sea level

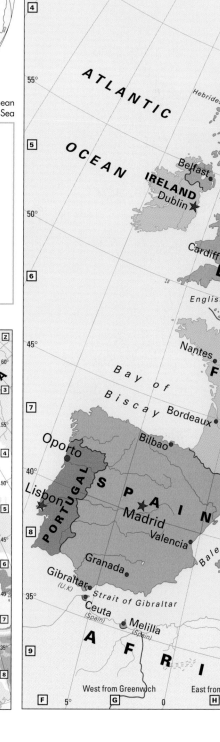

ARCTIC OCEAN

North Cape

Map information

Cities

★ Capital city

Ⓐ Index square - see index

Country boundary

Sea and lakes

MAP SCALE

This distance is 750 kilometres

or 500 miles

North

W — E

S

Lofoten
Islands

Narvik

Murmansk

White
Sea

Arkhangelsk

Arctic Circle

Shetland
Islands
(U.K.)

Trondheim

Bergen

N O R W A Y

S W E D E N

F I N L A N D

Gulf of Bothnia

North Dvina

Lake Onega

Perm

Lake Ladoga

R U S S I A

Oslo

Helsinki

Gulf of Finland

Tallinn

St. Petersburg

Volga

Kazan

Stockholm

ESTONIA

Gothenburg

Riga

Moscow

Samara

North
Sea

Baltic Sea

LATVIA

DENMARK
Copenhagen

LITHUANIA

(RUSSIA)

Vilnius

Minsk

BELARUS

Voronezh

NETHERLANDS
Amsterdam
The Hague

Hamburg

Gdansk

Vistula

Volga

Ural

Brussels

BELGIUM

Berlin

Warsaw

Elbe

GERMANY

POLAND

Kiev

Kharkov

Volgograd

Don

LUXEMBOURG

Frankfurt

Krakow

Oder

Lvov

U K R A I N E

Donetsk

Caspian Sea

Luxembourg

CZECH
REPUBLIC

Prague

Dnepropetrovsk

Rostov

Munich

Rhine

SLOVAK
REPUBLIC

Vienna

Bratislava

MOLDOVA

Krasnodar

Bern

LIECHTENSTEIN

AUSTRIA

Budapest

Chisinau

Odessa

Sea of
Azov

SWITZERLAND

HUNGARY

Crimea

Lyons

Ljubljana

SLOVENIA

Zagreb

CROATIA

Milan

Turin

I T A L Y

SAN
MARINO

BOSNIA-
HERZEGOVINA

Sarajevo

YUGOSLAVIA

Belgrade

ROMANIA

Bucharest

Danube

Sevastopol

B l a c k   S e a

GEORGIA

Tbilisi

AZERBAIJAN

Baku

Marseilles

MONACO

Adriatic Sea

BULGARIA

Sofia

Bosporus

ARMENIA

Yerevan

Corsica
(France)

Rome

Skopje

MACEDONIA

Istanbul

Naples

Tirane

ALBANIA

Sardinia
(Italy)

Mediterranean   Sea

Palermo

Sicily

G R E E C E

Aegean Sea

T U R K E Y

Ankara

A S I A

Izmir

Athens

Valletta

Crete

Nicosia

MALTA

CYPRUS

COPYRIGHT GEORGE PHILIP LTD

Largest countries – by area

(thousand square kilometres)

Russia 17,075
China 9,597
India 3,288

Largest countries – by population

(million people)

China 1,273
India 1,030
Indonesia 228
Russia 145

Largest cities

(million people)

Tokyo (JAPAN) 17.9
Mumbai (INDIA) 16.3
Shanghai (CHINA) 15.1
Kolkata (INDIA) 13.2
Beijing (CHINA) 12.4

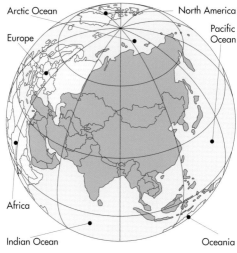

■ *Asia is the largest continent. It is twice the size of North America.*

■ *It is a continent of long rivers. Many of Asia's rivers are longer than Europe's longest rivers.*

■ *Asia contains well over half the world's population.*

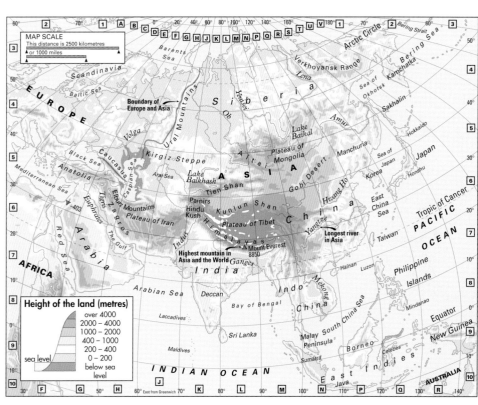

Height of the land (metres)

over 4000
2000 – 4000
1000 – 2000
400 – 1000
200 – 400
0 – 200
sea level   below sea level

MAP SCALE
This distance is 2500 kilometres
or 1000 miles

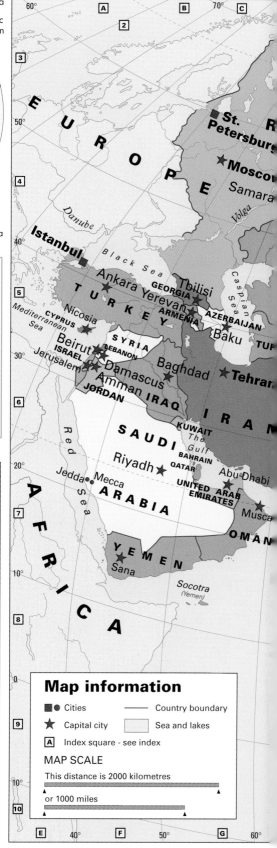

Map information

■● Cities   —— Country boundary

★ Capital city   ▭ Sea and lakes

Ⓐ Index square - see index

MAP SCALE

This distance is 2000 kilometres

or 1000 miles

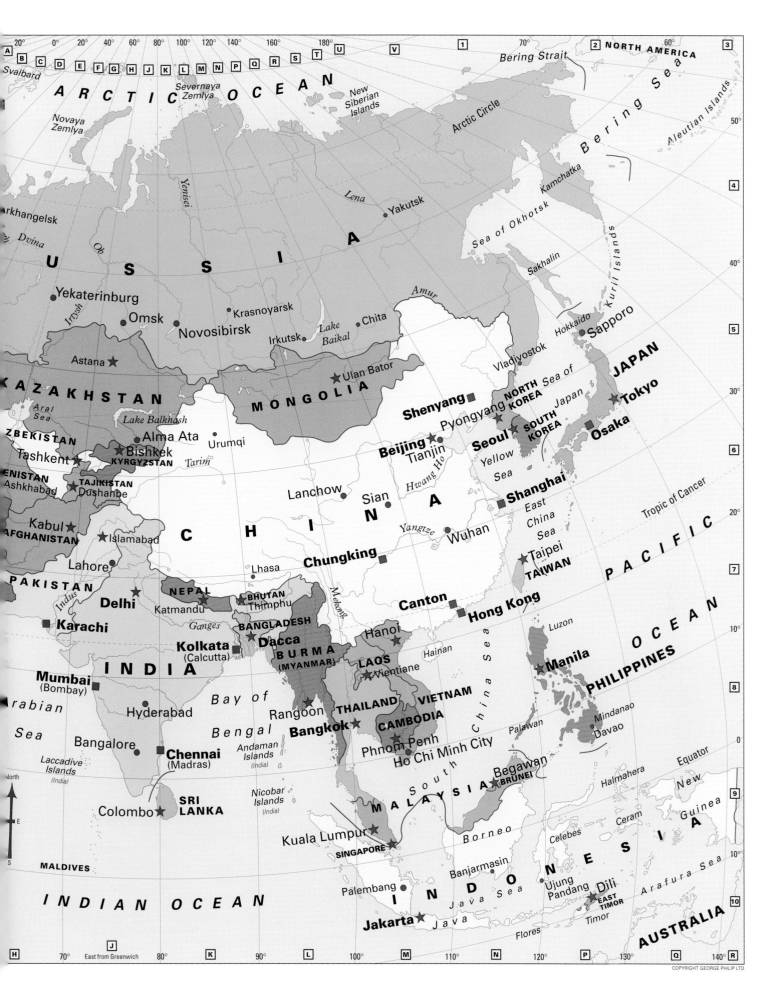

Africa

- Africa is the second largest continent. Asia is the largest.
- There are over 50 countries, some of them small in area and population. The population of Africa is growing more quickly than any other continent.
- Parts of Africa have a dry, desert climate. Other parts are tropical.
- The highest mountains run from north to south on the eastern side of Africa. The Great Rift Valley is a volcanic valley that was formed 10 to 20 million years ago by a crack in the Earth's crust. Mount Kenya and Mount Kilimanjaro are examples of old volcanoes in the area.
- The Sahara desert is the largest desert in the world.

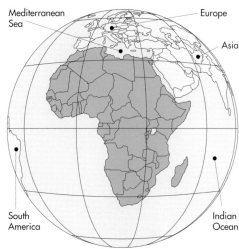

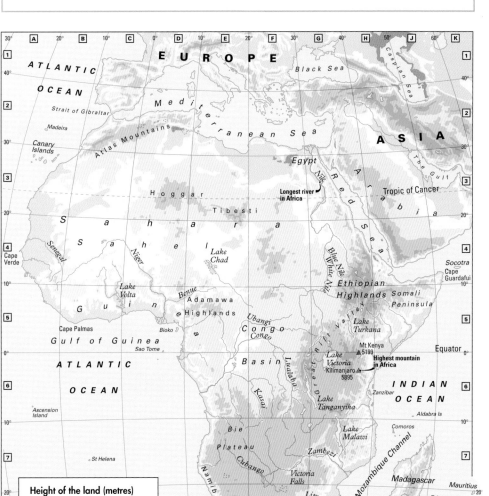

Largest countries – by area

(thousand square kilometres)

Sudan	2,506
Algeria	2,382
Congo (Dem. Rep.)	2,345
Libya	1,760
Chad	1,284
Niger	1,267

Largest countries – by population

(million people)

Nigeria	127
Egypt	70
Ethiopia	66
Congo (Dem. Rep.)	53
South Africa	44
Tanzania	36

Largest cities

(million people)

Lagos (NIGERIA)	10.2
Cairo (EGYPT)	9.7
Kinshasa (CONGO, DEM. REP.)	3.8
Alexandria (EGYPT)	3.4
Casablanca (MOROCCO)	2.9

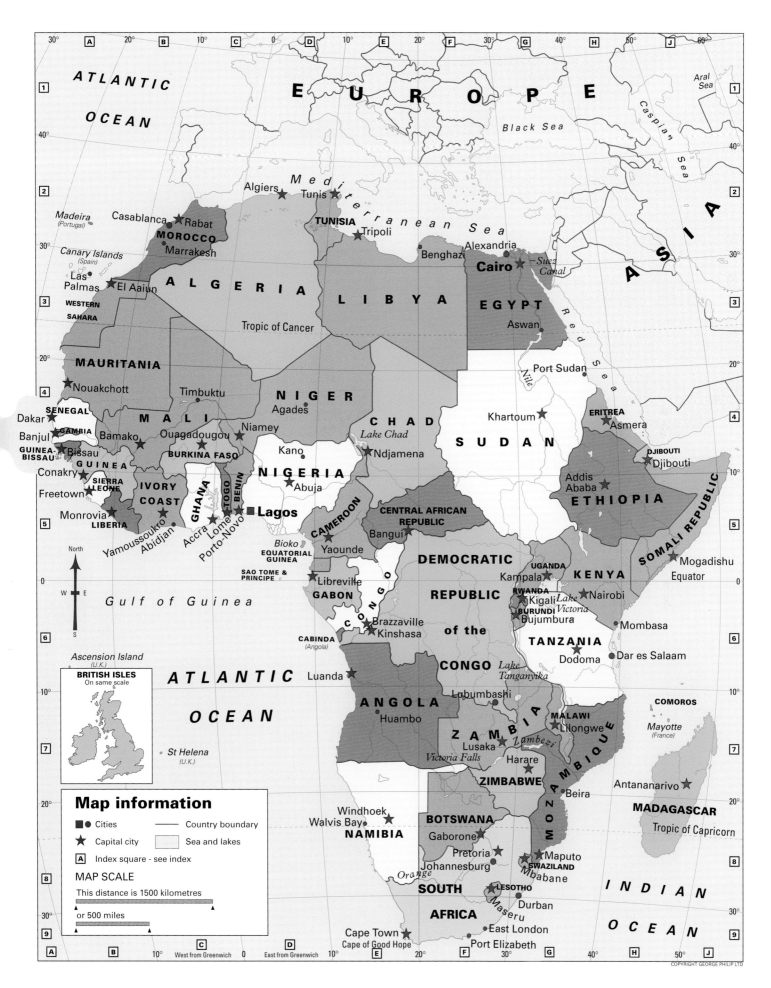

ATLANTIC

OCEAN

EUROPE

Aral Sea

Black Sea

Caspian Sea

Madeira (Portugal)

Algiers ★ Tunis

Mediterranean Sea

TUNISIA

Casablanca ★ Rabat ★ Tripoli

MOROCCO

Marrakesh

Benghazi ★ Alexandria

Canary Islands (Spain)

★ **Cairo**

Suez Canal

Las Palmas

★ El Aaiun

ALGERIA

LIBYA

EGYPT

WESTERN

SAHARA

Tropic of Cancer

Aswan

ASIA

Red Sea

Nile

Port Sudan

MAURITANIA

Timbuktu

NIGER

Agades

Khartoum ★

ERITREA

Asmera ★

★ Nouakchott

S U D A N

DJIBOUTI

Djibouti

SENEGAL

Dakar ★

CHAD

Lake Chad

Ndjamena

M A L I

Niamey

Bamako Ouagadougou ★

Addis Ababa ★

ETHIOPIA

Banjul

GAMBIA

Kano

GUINEA-

BISSAU

Bissau

BURKINA FASO

NIGERIA

GUINEA

Abuja ★

Conakry ★

SIERRA

LEONE

IVORY

■ **Lagos**

Freetown ★

COAST

GHANA

TOGO

BENIN

CAMEROON

CENTRAL AFRICAN REPUBLIC

Monrovia ★

Bangui ★

SOMALI REPUBLIC

LIBERIA

Accra Lome Porto-Novo

Yamoussoukro

Abidjan

UGANDA

Mogadishu ★

KENYA

Equator

Kampala ★

Bioko

Yaounde

EQUATORIAL GUINEA

Libreville ★

RWANDA

Kigali ★

Nairobi ★

North

DEMOCRATIC

Lake Victoria

SAO TOME & PRINCIPE

GABON

BURUNDI

Bujumbura ★

CONGO

Mombasa

Gulf of Guinea

REPUBLIC

W + E

Brazzaville ★

S

of the

TANZANIA

Dodoma ★

Dar es Salaam

Ascension Island (U.K.)

CABINDA (Angola)

Kinshasa ★

CONGO

Lake Tanganyika

BRITISH ISLES
On same scale

ATLANTIC

Luanda ★

Lubumbashi

COMOROS

OCEAN

Lusaka ★

MALAWI

Lilongwe ★

Mayotte (France)

ANGOLA

Huambo

ZAMBIA

Zambezi

St Helena *(U.K.)*

Harare ★

Victoria Falls

Antananarivo ★

MOZAMBIQUE

ZIMBABWE

Beira

Windhoek ★

MADAGASCAR

Tropic of Capricorn

Map information

■ ● Cities

— Country boundary

★ Capital city

Sea and lakes

Ⓐ Index square - see index

MAP SCALE

This distance is 1500 kilometres

or 500 miles

Walvis Bay

BOTSWANA

Gaborone ★

NAMIBIA

Pretoria ★

Maputo ★

Orange

Johannesburg

Mbabane ★

SWAZILAND

SOUTH

Maseru ★

LESOTHO

Durban

AFRICA

East London

INDIAN

Cape Town ★

Cape of Good Hope

Port Elizabeth

OCEAN

West from Greenwich East from Greenwich

COPYRIGHT GEORGE PHILIP LTD

55

- ■ *The continent is often called Oceania. It is made up of the huge island of Australia and thousands of other islands in the Pacific Ocean.*
- ■ *It is the smallest continent, only about a sixth the size of Asia.*
- ■ *The highest mountains are in the islands. Many of them are volcanic.*

Largest countries – by area

(thousand square kilometres)

Australia 7,687
Papua New Guinea 463
New Zealand 269

Largest countries – by population

(million people)

Australia 19
Papua New Guinea 5

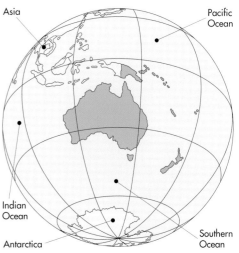

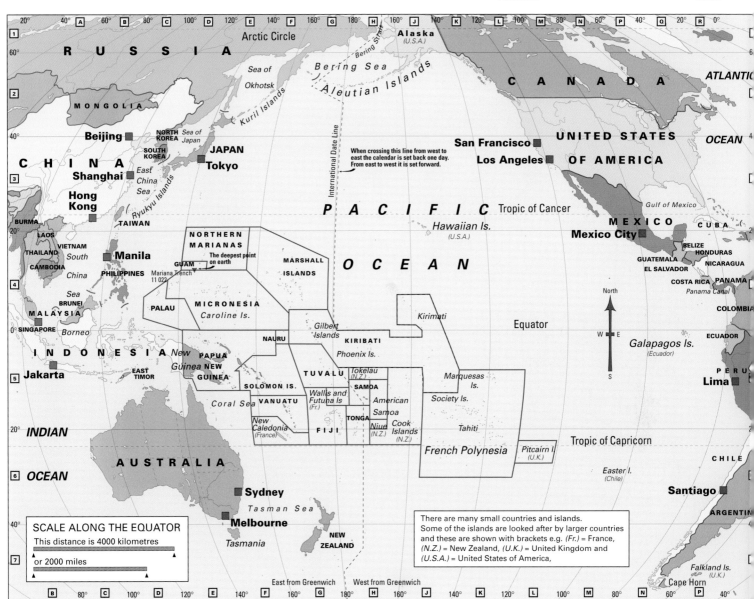

SCALE ALONG THE EQUATOR
This distance is 4000 kilometres
or 2000 miles

There are many small countries and islands.
Some of the islands are looked after by larger countries
and these are shown with brackets e.g. *(Fr.)* = France,
(N.Z.) = New Zealand, *(U.K.)* = United Kingdom and
(U.S.A.) = United States of America,

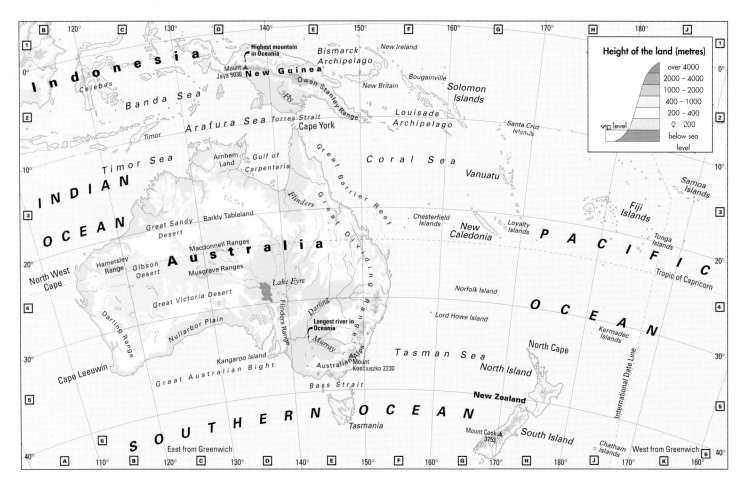

Height of the land (metres)

over 4000
2000 – 4000
1000 – 2000
400 – 1000
200 – 400
sea level 0 200
below sea
level

Indonesia
Celebes
Banda Sea
Timor
Highest mountain in Oceania
Mount Jaya 5030
New Guinea
Owen Stanley Range
Fly
Bismarck Archipelago
New Ireland
New Britain
Bougainville
Solomon Islands
Louisade Archipelago
Santa Cruz Islands
Arafura Sea
Torres Strait
Cape York
Coral Sea
Vanuatu
Samoa Islands
Timor Sea
Arnhem Land
Gulf of Carpentaria
Great Barrier Reef
Chesterfield Islands
New Caledonia
Loyalty Islands
Fiji Islands
Tonga Islands
INDIAN OCEAN
Great Sandy Desert
Barkly Tableland
Flinders
Great Dividing Range
Hamersley Range
Gibson Desert
Macdonnell Ranges
Musgrave Ranges
Australia
Lake Eyre
Tropic of Capricorn
North West Cape
Great Victoria Desert
Norfolk Island
PACIFIC
Darling Range
Nullarbor Plain
Flinders Range
Longest river in Oceania
Murray
Darling
Lord Howe Island
OCEAN
Kermadec Islands
Cape Leeuwin
Kangaroo Island
Great Australian Bight
Australian Alps
Mount Kosciuszko 2230
Tasman Sea
North Cape
North Island
New Zealand
Bass Strait
Tasmania
SOUTHERN OCEAN
Mount Cook 3753
South Island
Chatham Islands
East from Greenwich
West from Greenwich

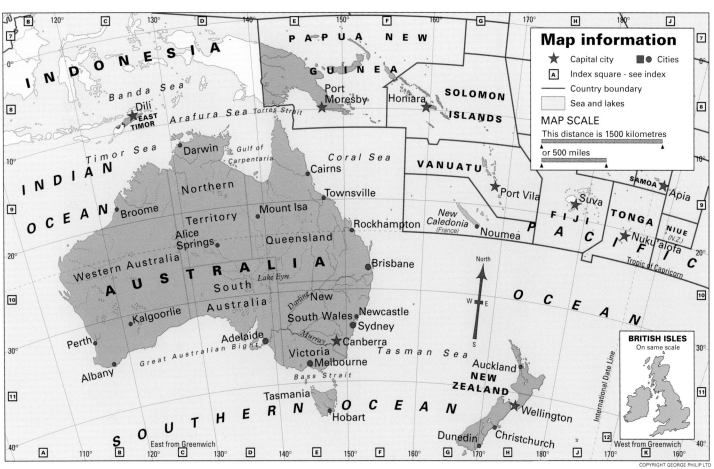

Map information

★ Capital city   ■● Cities

Ⓐ Index square - see index

— Country boundary

Sea and lakes

MAP SCALE
This distance is 1500 kilometres
or 500 miles

INDONESIA
Banda Sea
Dili
EAST TIMOR
Arafura Sea
Torres Strait
PAPUA NEW GUINEA
Port Moresby
Honiara
SOLOMON ISLANDS
Timor Sea
Darwin
Gulf of Carpentaria
Coral Sea
VANUATU
SAMOA
Apia
INDIAN OCEAN
Broome
Northern Territory
Cairns
Townsville
Port Vila
Suva
FIJI
TONGA
NIUE (N.Z.)
Alice Springs
Mount Isa
Rockhampton
New Caledonia (France)
Noumea
PACIFIC
Nuku'alofa
Western Australia
AUSTRALIA
Queensland
Lake Eyre
Brisbane
Tropic of Capricorn
South Australia
Darling
New South Wales
Newcastle
OCEAN
Kalgoorlie
Murray
Sydney
North
Perth
Adelaide
Canberra
Victoria
Tasman Sea
W E S
Auckland
NEW ZEALAND
Albany
Melbourne
Great Australian Bight
Bass Strait
Tasmania
Hobart
SOUTHERN OCEAN
Wellington
Dunedin
Christchurch
East from Greenwich
West from Greenwich
International Date Line

BRITISH ISLES
On same scale

COPYRIGHT GEORGE PHILIP LTD

57

- North America is the third largest continent. It is half the size of Asia. It stretches almost from the Equator to the North Pole.
- Three countries – Canada, the United States and Mexico – make up most of the continent.
- Greenland, the largest island in the world, is included within North America.

- In the east there are a series of large lakes. These are called the Great Lakes. A large waterfall called Niagara Falls is between Lake Erie and Lake Ontario. The St Lawrence river connects the Great Lakes with the Atlantic Ocean.
- There are mountains, volcanoes and high plains in the west, and rivers and lowlands in the east.

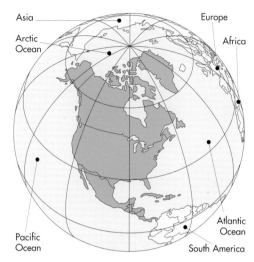

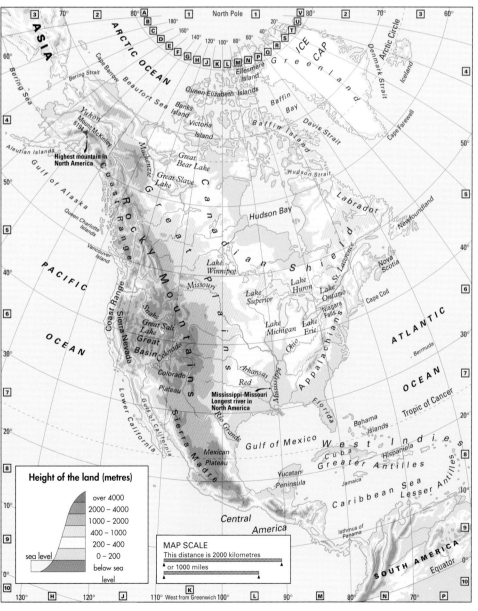

Largest countries – by area

(thousand square kilometres)

Canada	9,976
United States	9,373
Greenland	2,176
Mexico	1,958
Nicaragua	130
Honduras	112

Largest countries – by population

(million people)

United States	278
Mexico	102
Canada	32
Guatemala	13
Cuba	11
Dominican Republic	9

Largest cities

(million people)

New York (USA)	16.3
Mexico City (MEXICO)	15.6
Los Angeles (USA)	12.4
Chicago (USA)	7.6
Philadelphia (USA)	4.9

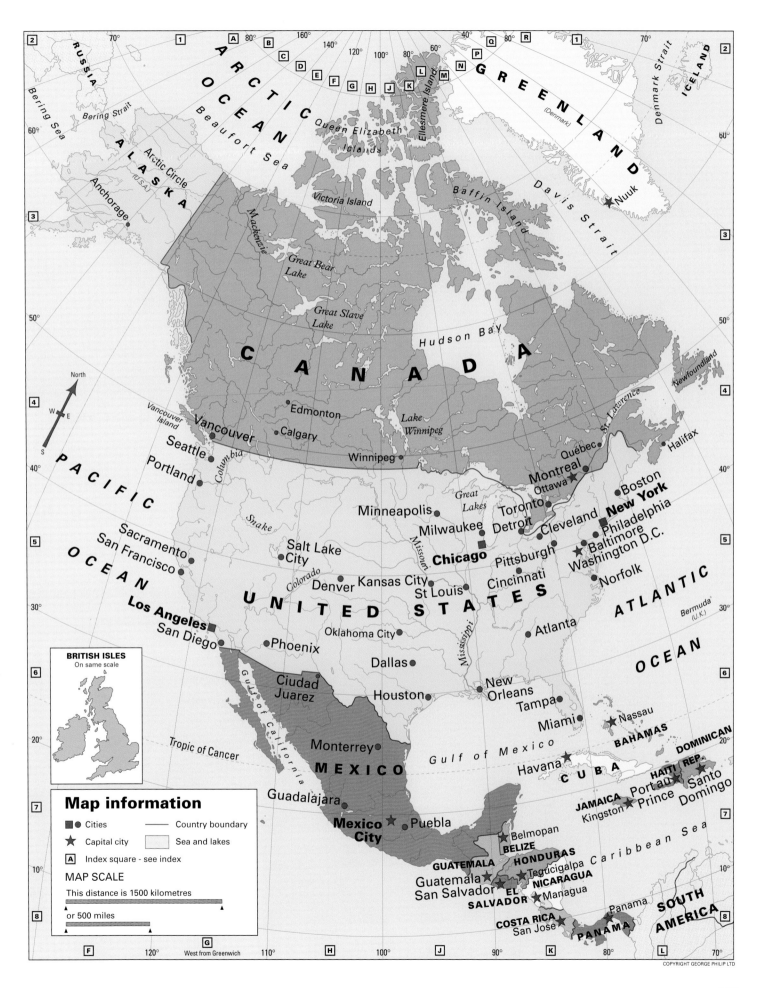

Map information

- Cities (dark square ■ and dot ●)
- ★ Capital city
- ⬛A Index square - see index
- Country boundary
- Sea and lakes

MAP SCALE

This distance is 1500 kilometres

or 500 miles

BRITISH ISLES
On same scale

RUSSIA

ARCTIC OCEAN

Bering Sea · Bering Strait · Beaufort Sea

ALASKA (USA) · Arctic Circle · Anchorage

Queen Elizabeth Islands · Ellesmere Island · Victoria Island · Baffin Island

GREENLAND (Denmark) · Denmark Strait · ICELAND · Davis Strait · ★ Nuuk

Mackenzie · Great Bear Lake · Great Slave Lake · Hudson Bay

C A N A D A

North · W E N S

Lake Winnipeg · St. Lawrence · Newfoundland

Vancouver Island · Vancouver · Edmonton · Calgary · Winnipeg · Québec · Halifax

Seattle · Columbia · Montreal · ★ Ottawa · Boston

Portland · Snake · Minneapolis · Toronto · Cleveland · **New York**

PACIFIC

Sacramento · San Francisco · Great Lakes · Milwaukee · Detroit · Philadelphia

O C E A N

Salt Lake City · Missouri · **Chicago** · Pittsburgh · Baltimore · ★ Washington D.C.

Denver · Colorado · Kansas City · St Louis · Cincinnati · Norfolk

U N I T E D   S T A T E S

ATLANTIC

Los Angeles · Oklahoma City · Atlanta · Bermuda (U.K.)

San Diego · Phoenix · Mississippi

Dallas · **O C E A N**

Ciudad Juarez · Houston · New Orleans

Gulf of California · Tampa · Miami · ★ Nassau

Tropic of Cancer · Monterrey · Gulf of Mexico · **BAHAMAS**

M E X I C O · ★ Havana · **CUBA** · **DOMINICAN REP.**

Guadalajara · **HAITI** · ★ Santo Domingo

Mexico City · ★ Puebla · **JAMACIA** · Port au Prince · **Caribbean Sea**

Kingston ★

★ Belmopan · **BELIZE**

GUATEMALA · **HONDURAS** · ★ Tegucigalpa

Guatemala ★ · **NICARAGUA**

San Salvador · **EL SALVADOR** · ★ Managua

COSTA RICA · ★ Panama · **SOUTH**

San Jose · **PANAMA** · **AMERICA**

COPYRIGHT GEORGE PHILIP LTD

59

South America

- The Amazon is the second longest river in the world. The Nile is the longest river, but more water flows from the Amazon into the ocean than from any other river.
- The range of mountains called the Andes runs for over 7,500 km from north to south on the western side of the continent. There are many volcanoes in the Andes.
- Lake Titicaca is the largest lake in the continent. It has an area of 8,300 sq km and is 3,800 metres above sea level.
- Spanish and Portuguese are the principal languages spoken in South America.
- Brazil is the largest country in area and population and is the richest in the continent.

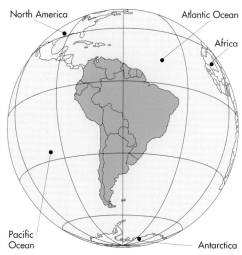

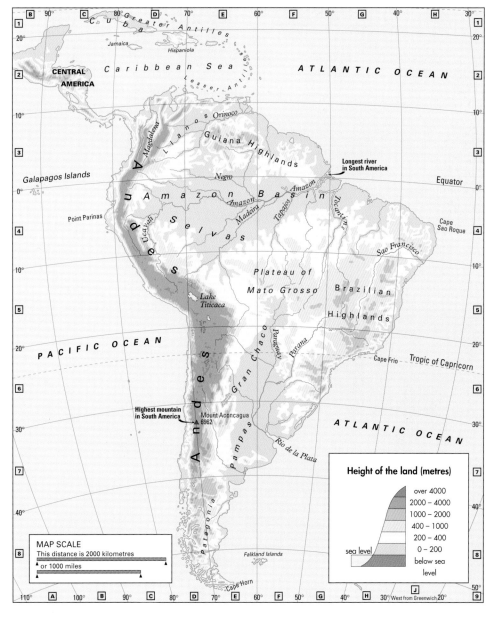

Largest countries – by area

(thousand square kilometres)

Brazil	8,512
Argentina	2,767
Peru	1,285
Colombia	1,139
Bolivia	1,099
Venezuela	912

Largest countries – by population

(million people)

Brazil	174
Colombia	40
Argentina	37
Peru	27
Venezuela	24
Chile	15

Largest cities

(million people)

Sao Paulo (BRAZIL)	16.4
Buenos Aires (ARGENTINA)	11.0
Rio de Janeiro (BRAZIL)	9.9
Lima (PERU)	6.6
Bogota (COLOMBIA)	6.0

MEXICO
BELIZE
GUATEMALA
HONDURAS
EL SALVADOR
NICARAGUA
COSTA RICA
PANAMA

Havana
CUBA
BAHAMAS
JAMAICA
HAITI
DOMINICAN REP.
Kingston
Port au Prince
Santo Domingo
PUERTO RICO
(U.S.A.)
VIRGIN IS.
(U.S.A.-U.K.)
ST KITTS-NEVIS
ANTIGUA & BARBUDA
GUADELOUPE
(France)
DOMINICA
MARTINIQUE (France)
ST LUCIA
ST VINCENT
NETHERLANDS
ANTILLES
GRENADA
BARBADOS

Caribbean Sea

Tegucigalpa
Managua
San Jose
Panama
Panama Canal

Barranquilla
Maracaibo
Valencia
Caracas
Port of Spain
TRINIDAD & TOBAGO

VENEZUELA
Orinoco

Medellin
Bogota
COLOMBIA
Cali

Georgetown
GUYANA
Paramaribo
SURINAME
FRENCH GUIANA
Cayenne

ATLANTIC OCEAN

Quito
ECUADOR
Guayaquil

Negro
Iquitos
Equator
Manaus
Amazon
Belem
Fortaleza

Galapagos Islands
(Ecuador)

Chiclayo
Trujillo
Ucayali

Madeira
Tapajos
Xingu
Tocantins
Sao Francisco
BRAZIL
Recife

PERU
Lima
Cuzco

PACIFIC

Arequipa
Lake Titicaca
La Paz
BOLIVIA
Sucre

Salvador
Brasilia
Goiania
Belo Horizonte

North
W E
S

Antofagasta
PARAGUAY
Asuncion
Sao Paulo
Rio de Janeiro
Tropic of Capricorn
Curitiba

OCEAN

CHILE
Tucuman
Cordoba
Rosario
URUGUAY
Montevideo
Buenos Aires
Rio de la Plata
Porto Alegre
ATLANTIC OCEAN

Valparaiso
Santiago
Concepcion
Juan Fernandez
(Chile)

ARGENTINA

Bahia Blanca

BRITISH ISLES
On same scale

Falkland Islands
(U.K.)
Stanley

Punta Arenas
Cape Horn

South Georgia
(U.K.)

Map information

■● Cities
★ Capital city
A Index square - see index

Country boundary
Sea and lakes

MAP SCALE

This distance is 1500 kilometres

or 500 miles

COPYRIGHT GEORGE PHILIP LTD

61

Polar Regions

The Polar Regions are the areas around the North Pole and the South Pole. The area around the North Pole is called the **Arctic** and the area around the South Pole is called the **Antarctic**. The sun never shines straight down on the Arctic or Antarctic so they are very cold – the coldest places on Earth. The Arctic consists of frozen water. Some parts of Northern Europe, North America and Asia are inside the Arctic Circle. A group of people called the Inuit live there.

Map information

- ■ Cities and towns
- ★ Capital cities
- ○ (Japan) Scientific stations in the Antarctic

Cross-section

Land covered in ice

Ice always in the sea

Ice sometimes in the sea

MAP SCALE
This distance is 1500 kilometres

or 500 miles

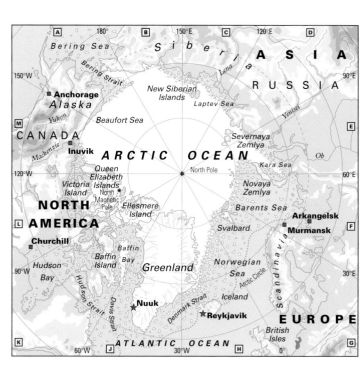

The Antarctic is a continent. It is bigger than Europe or Australia. There is no permanent population. Most of the land consists of ice which is thousands of metres thick. At the edges, chunks of ice break off to make icebergs. These float out to sea. The diagram below shows a cross-section through Antarctica between two of the scientific research stations, Siple and Casey. It shows how thick the ice is on the ice sheets.

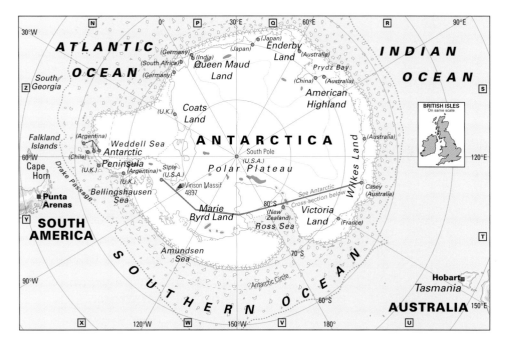

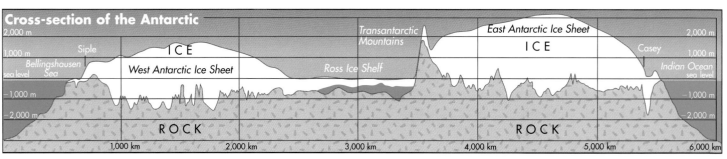

Cross-section of the Antarctic

— UK, Europe and the World —

United Nations

The UN is the largest international organization in the world. The headquarters are in New York and 191 countries are members. It was formed in 1945 to help solve world problems and to help keep world peace. The UN sends peacekeeping forces to areas where there are problems.

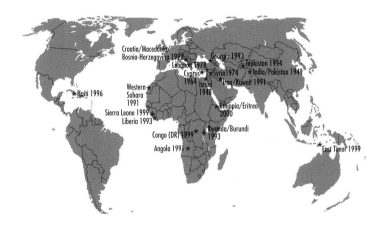

★ Peacekeeping forces with the year they were sent

European Union

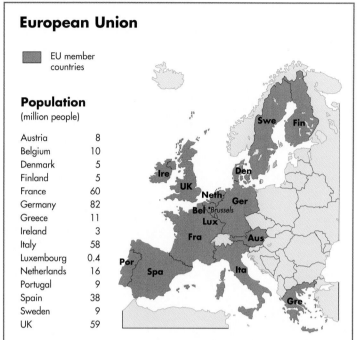

EU member countries

Population
(million people)

Austria	8
Belgium	10
Denmark	5
Finland	5
France	60
Germany	82
Greece	11
Ireland	3
Italy	58
Luxembourg	0.4
Netherlands	16
Portugal	9
Spain	38
Sweden	9
UK	59

The EU was first formed in 1951. Six countries were members. Now there are 15 countries in the EU. These countries meet to discuss agriculture, industry and trade as well as social and political issues. The headquarters are in Brussels. Cyprus, the Czech Republic, Estonia, Hungary, Latvia, Lithuania, Malta, Poland, Slovakia and Slovenia are expected to join the EU in 2004, with Bulgaria and Romania joining in 2007.

The Commonwealth

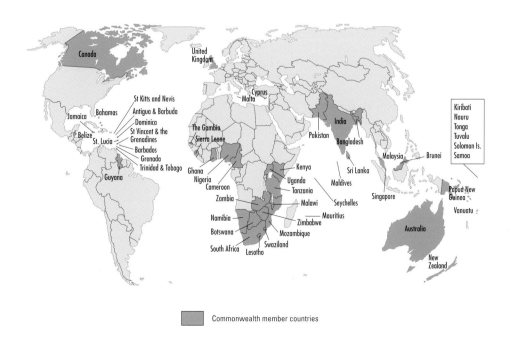

Commonwealth member countries

The Commonwealth is a group of 53 independent countries which used to belong to the British Empire. It is organized by a group of people called the Secretariat which is based in London. Queen Elizabeth II is the head of the Commonwealth. About every two years the heads of the different governments meet to discuss world problems. These meetings are held in different countries in the Commonwealth.

Index

Place	Page	Grid		Place	Page	Grid		Place	Page	Grid		Place	Page	Grid		Place	Page	Grid		Place	Page	Grid
Japan	53	R5		Luton	25	F6		Ness, Loch	26	D2		Poland	51	L5		Singapore	53	L8		Tralee	27	B4
Japan, Sea of	52	R4		Luxembourg	51	J6		Netherlands	51	H5		Port-au-Prince	59	L7		Skopje	51	M7		Trent, River	24	F4
Java	53	M9		Lvov	51	M6		New Guinea	57	D2		Port Laoise	27	C3		Skye	26	B2		Trinidad and		
Jersey	25	D8		Lyons	51	H6		New York	59	L4		Port Moresby	57	E8		Sligo	27	C2		Tobago	61	E2
Jerusalem	52	D5		Macedonia	51	M7		New Zealand	57	G11		Portland Bill	25	D7		Slovak Republic	51	L6		Tripoli	55	E2
John O'Groats	26	F1		Madagascar	55	H8		Newcastle	24	E3		Porto-Novo	55	C5		Slovenia	51	K6		Tunis	55	D2
Jordan	52	E6		Madrid	50	G8		Newfoundland	58	Q5		Portsmouth	25	F7		Snowdon	24	C4		Tunisia	55	D2
Kabul	53	H5		Majorca	50	H8		Newhaven	25	G7		Portugal	50	F8		Sofia	51	M7		Turin	51	J7
Kampala	55	F5		Malawi	55	G7		Newport	25	C6		Prague	51	L6		Solomon Islands	57	G8		Turkey	52	D5
Karachi	53	H6		Malaysia	53	M8		Newry	27	E2		Preston	24	C4		Somali Republic	55	H5		Turkmenistan	52	G5
Katmandu	53	J6		Mali	55	C4		Niagara Falls	58	N5		Pretoria	55	F8		South Africa	55	F8		Tuvalu	56	G5
Kazakhstan	53	G4		Malin Head	27	D1		Niamey	55	D4		Pyongyang	53	N4		South Downs	25	E6		Tweed, River	26	F4
Kenya	55	G5		Mallaig	26	C2		Nicaragua	59	K7		Pyrenees,				South Korea	53	P5		Tyne, River	24	E3
Khartoum	55	F4		Malta	51	K8		Nicosia	51	P8		mountains	50	H6		South Pole	62	S		Uganda	55	G5
Kiev	51	N5		Man, Isle of	24	B3		Niger	55	D4		Qatar	52	F6		Southampton	25	D7		Ukraine	51	M6
Kigali	55	G6		Managua	59	K7		Niger, River	54	D4		Québec	59	L4		Southend	25	G6		Ulan Bator	53	M4
Kilimanjaro, Mount	54	G6		Manchester	24	D4		Nigeria	55	D4		Quito	61	C4		Southern Ocean	62	X		United Arab		
Kilkenny	27	D4		Manila	53	P7		Nile, River	54	G3		Rabat	55	C2		Southern Uplands	26	D4		Emirates	52	F6
Killarney	27	B4		Maputo	55	G8		North Channel	27	F1		Rangoon	53	L7		Spain	50	F7		United Kingdom	50	G4
King's Lynn	25	G5		Marrakesh	55	C2		North Downs	25	F6		Reading	25	E6		Spey, River	26	E2		United States	59	G5
Kingston	59	K7		Marseilles	51	J7		North Korea	53	P4		Red Sea	54	G3		Sri Lanka	53	K8		Ural Mountains	50	W1
Kinnaird Head	26	G2		Maseru	55	F9		North Minch	26	B2		Ree, Lough	27	D3		Stafford	25	D5		Uruguay	61	F7
Kinshasa	55	E6		Mask, Lough	27	B3		North Pole	62	E		Réunion	54	J8		Stirling	26	D3		Uzbekistan	53	G4
Kintyre	26	C4		Mauritania	55	B4		North Sea	50	J3		Reykjavik	50	C3		Stockholm	51	K4		Valletta	51	K8
Kiribati	56	H5		Mauritius	54	J7		North West				Rhine, River	50	K4		Stoke on Trent	25	D4		Vancouver	59	F3
Kirkwall	26	J7		Mbabane	55	G8		Highlands	26	C3		Rhone, River	50	J6		Stornoway	26	B1		Vanuatu	57	F9
Knockmealdown				McKinley, Mount	58	E3		North York Moors	24	E3		Riga	51	N4		Stranraer	26	D5		Venezuela	61	D3
Mountains	27	C4		Mecca	52	F6		Northampton	25	F5		Rio de Janeiro	61	G6		Sucre	61	E5		Verde, Cape	54	B4
Kolkata	53	K6		Mediterranean				Northern Ireland	27	D2		Riyadh	52	F6		Sudan	55	F4		Victoria Falls	54	F7
Kuala Lumpur	53	L8		Sea	50	J7		Norway	51	J3		Rocky Mountains	58	H3		Suez Canal	55	G2		Victoria, Lake	54	G6
Kuwait	52	F6		Mekong, River	52	N7		Norwich	25	G5		Romania	51	M6		Sunderland	24	E3		Vienna	51	K6
Kyle of Lochalsh	26	C2		Merthyr Tydfil	25	C6		Nottingham	25	E5		Rome	51	K7		Superior, Lake	58	L5		Vientiane	53	M7
Kyrgyzstan	53	J4		Mexico	59	H6		Nouakchott	55	B4		Rosslare	27	E4		Suriname	61	F3		Vietnam	53	M7
La Paz	61	E5		Mexico City	59	H7		Nuuk	59	P2		Russia	52	F2		Swansea	25	B6		Vilnius	51	N5
Lagos	55	D5		Mexico, Gulf of	58	L7		Oban	26	C3		Rwanda	55	F6		Swaziland	55	G8		Wales	25	B5
Lake District	24	C3		Miami	59	K6		Omagh	27	D2		Sahara, desert	54	B4		Sweden	51	K4		Warsaw	51	L5
Land's End	25	A8		Michigan, Lake	58	L5		Oman	52	G6		St George's				Switzerland	51	J6		Wash, The	25	G5
Laos	53	M7		Middlesbrough	24	E3		Ontario, Lake	58	N5		Channel	27	E5		Sydney	57	F11		Washington D.C.	59	L5
Lapland	50	N1		Milan	51	J6		Oporto	50	E7		St Lucia	61	E2		Syria	52	E5		Waterford	27	D4
Larne	27	F2		Milford Haven	25	B6		Orange, River	54	E8		St Petersburg	51	P4		Taipei	53	P6		Weald, The	25	F6
Latvia	51	M4		Milton Keynes	25	F5		Orinoco, River	60	E3		Salisbury Plain	25	D6		Taiwan	53	P6		Wellington	57	H12
Lebanon	52	E5		Minsk	51	N5		Orkney Islands	26	J7		Samoa	57	J9		Tajikistan	53	H5		Western Sahara	55	B3
Leeds	24	E4		Mississippi, River	58	L6		Oslo	51	J3		San Francisco	59	E5		Tallinn	51	N4		Westport	27	A3
Leicester	25	E5		Missouri, River	58	K5		Ottawa	59	K4		San Jose	59	K8		Tanganyika, Lake	54	G6		Wexford	27	E4
Lerwick	26	H6		Mogadishu	55	H5		Ouagadougou	55	C4		San Marino	51	K7		Tanzania	55	G6		Weymouth	25	C7
Lesotho	55	F8		Moldova	51	N6		Ouse, River (Cam.)	25	F5		San Salvador	59	J7		Tashkent	53	H4		Wick	26	E1
Lewis	26	B1		Monaco	51	J7		Ouse, River (Yorks)	24	E3		Sana	52	F7		Tasmania	57	D12		Wicklow Head	27	F4
Liberia	55	B5		Mongolia	53	L4		Ox Mountains	27	C2		Santiago	61	D7		Taunton	25	C6		Wicklow		
Libreville	55	E6		Monrovia	55	B5		Oxford	25	E6		Santo Domingo	59	L7		Tay, River	26	E3		Mountains	27	E3
Libya	55	E3		Montevideo	61	F7		Pacific Ocean	56	G3		Sao Paulo	61	F6		Tbilisi	52	F4		Wight, Isle of	25	E7
Liffey, River	27	E3		Montreal	59	K4		Pakistan	53	H6		Sarajevo	51	L7		Tegucigalpa	59	K7		Windhoek	55	E8
Lilongwe	55	G7		Moray Firth	26	E2		Panama	59	K8		Sardinia	51	J7		Tehran	52	G5		Winnipeg	59	H4
Lima	61	C5		Morocco	55	C2		Panama Canal	61	D2		Saudi Arabia	52	F6		Thailand	53	L7		Wolverhampton	25	C5
Limerick	27	C4		Moscow	51	Q4		Papua New				Scafell	24	C3		Thames, River	25	E6		Worcester	25	D5
Lincoln	24	F4		Mourne				Guinea	57	E8		Scarborough	24	F3		The Hague	51	J5		Wrath, Cape	26	C1
Lincolnshire Wolds	24	F4		Mountains	27	E2		Paraguay	61	E6		Scilly Isles	25	A8		Thimphu	53	L6		Wye, River	25	D5
Lisbon	50	F8		Mozambique	55	G8		Paramaribo	61	F3		Scotland	26	C3		Thurso	26	D1		Yangtze, River	52	N6
Lithuania	51	M4		Mull	26	B3		Paris	50	G6		Senegal	55	B4		Tibet, Plateau of	52	L5		Yamoussoukro	55	B5
Liverpool	24	C4		Mumbai	53	H7		Peak District	24	E4		Seoul	53	P5		Tigris, River	52	G5		Yaounde	55	E5
Ljubljana	51	K6		Muscat	52	G6		Pennines	24	D3		Severn, River	25	D5		Timbuktu	55	C4		Yemen	52	F7
Lome	55	C5		Nairobi	55	G6		Penzance	25	A7		Shanghai	53	P5		Tirane	51	L7		Yerevan	52	E4
Lomond, Loch	26	D3		Namibia	55	E8		Perth	26	E3		Shannon, River	27	C3		Titicaca, Lake	60	E5		York	24	E4
London	25	G6		Navan	27	D3		Peru	61	D5		Sheffield	24	E4		Togo	55	D5		Yugoslavia	51	L6
Londonderry	27	D2		Ndjamena	55	E4		Peterborough	25	F5		Shetland Islands	26	H6		Tokyo	53	R5		Zagreb	51	L6
Los Angeles	59	F5		Neagh, Lough	27	E2		Philippines	53	P7		Shrewsbury	25	C5		Tonga	57	J9		Zambezi, River	54	G7
Luanda	55	D6		Nene, River	25	F5		Phnom Penh	53	M7		Sierra Leone	55	B5		Torbay	25	C7		Zambia	55	F7
Lusaka	55	F7		Nepal	53	K6		Plymouth	25	B7						Toronto	59	K4		Zimbabwe	55	F7